"If we have promised more than our economy has the ability to deliver to retirees without unduly diminishing real income gains of workers, as I fear we may have, we must recalibrate our public programs so that pending retirees have time to adjust through other channels.

If we delay, the adjustments could be abrupt and painful."

Alan Greenspan, Chairman
Federal Reserve Board
Jackson Hole, Wyoming
August 27, 2004 [1]

THE REAL TIME BOMB

The Aging of America and The Retirement Crisis

David Hoefferle

Advisors Publishing

The following is the commentary of David Hoefferle, and should not be construed as investment advice. This opinion is subject to change with market conditions and is not meant as a market forecast. Please consult your financial advisor for more information.

Securities offered through David Hoefferle doing business as UNITED FINANCIAL CENTER, LLC, as a Registered Representative and Investment Advisor Representative of Advantage Capital Corporation Member NASD, SIPC & Member of AIG Advisor Group.

United Financial Center, LLC
P.O. Box 30099
Tucson, AZ 85751-0099
1-877-953-1040
www.unitedfinancial.net
book@unitedfinancial.net

Printed in the United States of America by U.S. Press & Graphics, Tucson, Arizona.

Design by Steve McMackin, Impulse Designs

Published by **Advisors Publishing**

ISBN 0-9764739-0-9

2005

To Rena

FIRST...

Some of my closest friends have said, "Aren't you being too negative? People want to increase their wealth, not worry about losing it."

I understand what they mean, but I see finances from a different perspective. My message is simple; it's about both making more money and keeping what you make.

Let me assure you, I am excited about the future! History proves nearly 80% of our lives are the best of times. Sure there are minor financial corrections on occasion, but life in general is positive.

Every once in a while, though, there is a period when everything seems to fall apart. If you knew it was coming, if you had the chance, wouldn't you be wise to get ready for such a time?

This warning voice asks you to see the big picture, both the good and the bad. If you do, you will be one of the few who will weather the financial problems that can come your way.

With proper modifications the distressing financial outcome of "The Real Time Bomb" will never happen. I wish this was the end of the story. It would save everyone a lot of time and anxiety. But the corrections may not be made fast enough, so it is essential you know the facts and what you can do to prepare.

This book is a result of the many questions I receive as a Financial and Tax Consultant. As my clients visit with me their concerns often turn from saving money on taxes to what I think will happen to their investments in the future. I didn't graduate summa cum laude, near the top of my class, for nothing. I find great satisfaction in understanding the finer points of financial planning and enjoy communicating that knowledge. Yet as I go into an in-depth explanation, sometimes it takes me a while before I see my clients' eyes glaze over and I finally realize they didn't want to eat both the bull and the bear. They just wanted to know if they should get out of the way if one of them charged!

By the time you finish reading I hope you will understand there is a reason to have an investment advisor and to be ready for whatever the future holds. I truly hope that none of the potential bad news happens. But *if* it does you will never be able to say you weren't warned. If the negative economic forecast does come about and you have tried to get ready, you will at least have something to salvage from the wreckage. If it does not take place then you are in luck. If our government leaders have done their job and protected us from the potential gloom and doom, then you may have saved a lot of money and have put enough aside for your happy retirement.

However, if you sit back and expect the government to protect you or pay for your carefree retirement, you may be very disappointed.

I challenge you to do something about it.

Finally, this book is the result of many who have provided exceptional assistance. My wife, Rena, has been extremely patient helping with each page and gave up her vacation. My son, Ryan, has given his advice. My daughter, Andrea, was accommodating since she just received her learner's permit and wanted me to teach her to drive, but understood that I was driven to tell this story. My staff has also been of great help as I have spent many hours at my computer. Lisa Harter, Mindy Bennett, Erik Ludvickson, Jim Marsh, and others kindly sat and listened to my ideas, gave feedback, helped proofread, and provided valuable research help. Steve McMackin designed the cover and layout, Rachel Garman edited, and Barbara Guzman of the Advantage Capital Corporation Compliance Department provided excellent service making corrections as needed. I am grateful for their support.

Contents

01:00

Watch Out!

“Thanks! You've left me totally depressed. Now what do I do?”

“Well,” I said matter-of-factly, back-peddling a little, “I hope I am wrong!”

My client probably figured I should have the answer because I am the financial and tax expert. He knew I was associate faculty at the University of Phoenix where I teach financial planning courses.

This wasn’t academic rhetoric. This was a good friend, asking a very serious question. He wanted to know what he should do.

His question was a good one. “When it comes to my investments, what should I do to prepare for the long-term?”

My answer didn’t happen to be the optimistic one he was expecting, especially when he was looking forward to years of comfort and leisure during his long anticipated retirement. I told him why he should reconsider his plans for the future. I didn't mean to be pessimistic or to sound like a doomsday prophet. I only presented the facts.

When I finished, I reminded him that I was only the messenger. I wasn't the one saying these things. I was the reporter, gathering the information, presenting the opinions of others, and focusing in on the potential outcome in a way few advisors want to think about because it means a drastic change to their potential earnings.

"Now," I said, "I don't have a crystal ball; I don't know what will happen in the future. In fact I hope I am wrong!" I told him, "And if I am wrong there will be no harm done. You will have wisely prepared and diversified your investments. But if I am right, this information may be the most important you could ever use to prepare for the unknown that lies ahead."

That same week, I was invited to talk about budgeting money to a class of soon-to-be graduating seniors from a local university. They came to learn how to manage their finances and prepare for their positive future. Instead, I presented the dismal facts once more. As they sat in their classroom, staring at me and the note-filled white board, I could see from their sullen faces that the story of realism was not a popular one. But I could tell that I had their attention.

I was about ready to wrap up the portion of my presentation dealing with the grim facts of the future when I said, "So, all I can tell you is this: if you don't listen, if I am right and you don't do what I tell you, then shame on you!" I could tell by their nervous laughter I had struck a chord.

My message: If all the components come together at one time like some of our best economists are warning, we could have a "perfect storm" on our hands which could leave a desolate financial landscape in its wake.

Tell It Like It Is!

The first half of my career was spent as a journalist repeating back to the public what I heard and saw. As a television news anchor and reporter, and a brief stint as a weathercaster, I learned how to watch and listen, and then try to communicate what I saw in an unbiased story.

My first news director, taking a marker to my report, pounded the message out loud and clear: "Keep It Simple!" Don't worry about making the story bigger than it is, he would remind me. Just describe the facts. And above all don't make it up because eventually the truth will be made known.

Since that time, I have learned from some of the best minds in the investment industry. Working for nearly twenty years as a financial and tax consultant, it is clear to me that my job is to communicate the not-so-obvious: there's a financial storm on the horizon!

So when my friend asked, "What would you recommend I do to prepare for the future?" I couldn't hold back. I had to tell him what I saw coming. I would be at fault if I didn't inform him of the facts and the financial dangers that lie ahead. I felt it was my obligation to be a warning voice.

When hundreds of people show up at my seminars, I have been intrigued by their deer-in-the-headlight response. These people, many of whom have already been through a lot in their lives (a few wars, a number of recessions, and for some, the Great Depression), looked at me with that "it's-not-going-to-happen-in-my-lifetime" look. But no one questioned the facts as presented.

Now, my license from the National Association of Securities Dealers (NASD) requires me to tell you I have gathered this information from some of the most reputable sources I know. I am not speaking on my own, nor am I attempting to foretell future trends of the stock market and world economy.

Scary!

Years ago, my wife and I always got a hearty laugh whenever our three-year old son was startled. Even if it was a mild-mannered classic Disney animated movie, he would slowly turn, with wide-eyed wonder, looking for some reassurance from his parents, and deliberately say, "s-s-s-SCeery!"

As I review the future and what it holds for us, all I can say is, "Scary!" But for us, there will be no one to offer any loving reassurance. The effects of the real world may soon be upon us.

Normally, I try to be optimistic about the future. I want to believe there will be a rainbow at the end of the storm but listening to the economic scholars of our time and collecting what seemed to be the most vital information has left me piecing together the following puzzle:

> In the years leading up to 2010 (give or take a few years), we should see a period of economic prosperity. There could be any number of surprises along the way which could derail this growth.
>
> However, this period may be followed by a prolonged Bear Market which has the potential to last for more than a decade. Some of the financial wizards of our day have even suggested this may result in the word that should not be named. A depression could actually be in the making and some are saying it will be worse than the Great Depression of the 1930s[2].

This scenario may never happen. There are many variables that could correct the financial course we are on. But for now, the future appears downright scary.

There is one part of this scenario that will happen as sure as the sun will come up tomorrow. And it's a series of events that no one has control over. It's a real, honest-to-goodness, ticking away time-bomb that no one can stop. We're all growing older and no one wants to die, at least not when we are healthy and happy. This hang-on-at-all-cost attitude is catching up with us. Someone is going to pay, whether it is us or our children.

What "Golden Years"? Old-Age Stinks!

Does anyone know if Patrick Henry really meant it when he dramatically proclaimed, "Give me liberty or give me death!"

Okay, take your pick: life or death.

Imagine being marched to some form of death machine, whether it is the guillotine, electric chair, or whatever. If you are like most people, you are going to do all you can to save your life.

Now, imagine the clock ticking, marching you second by second to the grave. Once again, when given a choice, especially when you know there are life-saving or extending options available, you are going to do all you can to avoid pain and the uncomfortable realization that you are taking your last breath. Whether it is the chance of cancer, heart disease, or any other malady that ends in death patients line the physician's waiting rooms looking for some way to advance life, liberty, and the pursuit of happiness.

Death is not an acceptable option. Few people want to die. Even those who say they want to be put out of their misery rather than live through a prolonged illness will often cling to every last breath.

Not that it is wrong – and let me make this perfectly clear, I want to extend my life as long as I can - but this survival instinct may be the very thing that is our financial undoing. This natural desire to comfortably live long and prosper, with a healthy dosage of the almighty dollar, is the driving force behind the medical industry and its mission to save lives.

As lives are extended, people often live in a frail, unproductive state for ten or more years. That is up to one eighth of your life! Who is going to take care of you? Where are you going to get the money to have someone take care of you? Since few people are financially prepared, where is the government going to come up with the money to pay for the comfortable care of millions of deserving poor?

It is time for me to get personal for a moment.

As a tax and investment adviser, I have specialized in retirement and estate planning. My clients spend valuable time making plans for their future when they are no longer able to care for themselves. They also map out how their assets will be distributed among their beneficiaries. I do not know of one person who is looking forward to death. And yet, excessive medical expenses, uncontrollable pain and illness, loneliness, and loss of both memory and bodily function cause some people to want to die before they become financial, physical and emotional drains on their family.

When we were younger, my parents asked me and my wife to keep them out of nursing homes as long as we could. Without understanding what we were getting ourselves into, we agreed. My father suddenly died in the early 1990s, at the age of 72, leaving us to care for my aging mother, who had health issues from a fall on the ice ten years earlier. The first few years were tolerable as she lived with us and we raised our four children. Then we learned the not-so-surprising news that my mother had dementia and was in the early stages of Alzheimer's.

Luckily my mother purchased long-term care insurance when she was still eligible. When it was needed the insurance plan provided the money to pay for a considerate caretaker to assist my mother at home. But that money lasts for only part of the day. For years now, my family and I have been responsible for my mother's most basic needs. There have been many times when we asked how long we can continue to care for her. In her advanced years, even though her heart is strong, her mind continues to fail. Our answer is based solely on our ability, not our love or our selfishness.

Selflessness is not easy. This type of commitment is not something I would readily encourage others to undertake. More than a dozen years have passed, with seldom a week going by when I do not remind myself that she cared for me for years and I have the obligation to do the same for her as long as we can.

Because of this experience, I know firsthand what aging is all about. Perhaps the greatest apprehension I have about the future is not financial uncertainty. My concern is that each of us needs to prepare for the inevitable aging process and what will happen when we are no longer able to care for ourselves or our loved ones.

This irreversible aging process, and the fact that millions of us are getting older all at once, will change America and our lives as we know it. You can't stop time or change what you should have done, but you can organize your financial affairs before it is too late.

Even while the sun shines and all seems secure, there are dark, ominous clouds gathering on the horizon. As overwhelming as the potential problems are, each of us must look for the rainbow after the coming financial storm.

So, what should you do?

Just Do It!

The next few pages are not intended to be the final word. This book is not designed to provide a one-size-fits-all answer. It is intended to make you aware of the possibilities that may occur and provide some general ideas that you should consider as you take the necessary financial steps to prepare for these potential developments.

What I hope you will do is watch out and act on this one old truism:

> If you are prepared, you shall not fear!

I hope I am wrong. I hope that another depression never happens. I hope that the stock market and our economy keep going up forever. But we know that is not realistic.

Frankly, if I am wrong, and a downturn in the market does not happen in the second decade of the century, you will be much further ahead. At the very least, if you follow my advice you will be ready. And that's where you want to be anyway, right?

Your kindergarten teacher showed you where to find the exits in case of a fire. She did not want you to worry that a fire could occur. But knowing about the precautions and escape plans made everyone feel better.

So, do you have a financial escape route planned? My advice is to prepare <u>now</u> by looking into the possibilities and determine what your options should be.

Let me stress the fact that this is <u>not</u> a financial prediction that some particular event will happen in our future. I know pessimistic prophecies seldom come true. Instead, I am reporting on the trends, alerting you of the potential dangers ahead, and providing sound recommendations how you can prepare and come out ahead no matter what the future brings.

Finally, if I believed my clients <u>could</u> lose money, what kind of financial advisor would I be if I didn't say what concerned me? My attitude is simple. If you don't listen, that is your choice. At least I have informed you. It is now up to you.

This is why you must continue reading on.

02:00

Predicting Our Puzzling Future

Looking into the future is like placing pieces of an intricate puzzle in their proper positions while blindfolded. While it is easy to make broad sweeping statements that few predictions ever come true, it doesn't mean predictions are *never* right.

Here is one simple and quite obvious exercise that will prove some forecasts will *always* come true.

Assume a family decides to take a weekend drive from Phoenix, Arizona to Los Angeles, California. Part of the trip includes a hundred mile strip of lonely desert with no service stations between. Their vehicle has less than a quarter tank of gas. There is an obvious conclusion: they could run out of fuel. This prediction would probably come true with unfortunate results.

Now imagine a checking account that is close to running out of money. Payday is still two weeks away. Yet food and utilities still need to be paid. Writing a check without proper preparation could also result in an unhappy ending.

Using this same form of deductive reasoning can allow you to look into the future and determine a plausible outcome when it comes to our national economy and how it will affect you. Most people, however, have not taken the time to become aware of the warning signs.

Researchers have found investors seldom have the patience to look more than five years into the future and are very short-sighted when it comes to looking at the facts. For this very reason most analysts don't even bother with trying to get investors to pay attention.[3]

Not a Pretty Picture

There are a number of factors that may lead to an uncertain future. There is no need to assume this is secret information. Each of the factors has been thoroughly discussed in open forums. In fact, most people will be familiar with the topics. And yet this joining together of bad news will probably not be analyzed until after the disaster occurs.

What is this convergence you ask?

Here are some of the larger pieces of the social and economic puzzle, this dilemma in the making:

- More than 77 million retirees in 18 years;
- The potential doubling of social security and medicare taxes;
- Excessive national and personal debt;

- The possibility of a real estate bubble;
- The continuing polarization of the world's social structure partly due to both fanatics and power hungry emerging nations;
- The world's population explosion and subsequent implosion in some countries;
- The potential destabilization of our "guaranteed" banking structure warned about by the very organization designed and set up to protect our money, the FDIC (Federal Deposit Insurance Corporation), which would require massive amounts of taxpayer assistance;
- And finally, greed and fear, the balance of which is respectfully called "Caution," but the escalated combination of which can lead to frenzy or panic.

Look at any one issue by itself and most people will say, "So what's new? I've heard it all before!" But bring them all together at once and see what happens!

Topics of this nature have seldom been trumpeted to the public because bad news of this sort has never been well received in the media. Or, if the matter has been discussed, it has been poorly promoted and quickly forgotten.

There is no easy fix. Because the tale can't be spun in a short news report, there is no interest to make it into a full-fledged news special. No advertiser would be interested in spending large amounts of money to attach their name to such a depressing report.

In addition, there are too many not-so-little problems for our local and national leaders to fix in today's complex world. Normally, they are chasing after the issues that concern their constituents today. When it comes to their financial future most people haven't gotten it in their heads that their gravy train may some day come to a sudden end.

Why haven't you heard more about this? The bottom line is that it just doesn't make a lot of money and it actually requires some expensive decisions that most corporate and government leaders don't want to address, at least not now.

Despite the prediction by dozens of qualified analysts and economists, until you and a lot more people speak up and demand something be done about the looming financial crisis, there's a good chance that our runaway economy will continue to head towards a possible crash of global proportions.

What, Me Worry?

Before we look at the worrisome puzzle pieces of our future we need to be reminded of the underlying emotions driving our economy. Greed and fear are the two divergent feelings that often override self-control and rational thinking. These emotions provide the drive behind the action, but without balance, we can lose sight of making reasonable decisions.

Economic greed was described in 1996 by Alan Greenspan, Chairman of the United States Federal Reserve, when he warned of the "irrational exuberance" that was driving the markets.[4] When government, corporations, and the investing public all become wound up in the rush for riches, they often forget to take an occasional step back to see where their actions are leading.

Greed is also a factor causing investors to be unsure of their next move. This uncertainty makes people act irrationally bouncing back and forth between greed and fear. Although normally cautious, many investors overreact to keep their nest egg. Worry causes the fear, but greed brings on the wild-eyed Midas-like desire to hold on to every last penny. Clutching their hoard, savers falsely trust that their FDIC "guarantee" means their money is never at risk. But as seen later on there are risks and the only true guarantee is spreading out assets in a number of investment vehicles, which is also known as diversification.

Franklin D. Roosevelt, in his 1932 inaugural address, warned that "the only thing we have to fear is fear itself." He described fear as "nameless, unreasoning, unjustified terror which paralyzes needed efforts" to go forward.[5] But when the herd stampedes it is difficult to stop.

At a time when the nation's morale couldn't get any lower, President Roosevelt had the courage to be optimistic and positive. While in the midst of national despair, and with the noble desire to spur the people forward, he said, "This great Nation will endure as it has endured, will revive and will prosper."[6]

Now, after many years of a prosperous economy, greed and fear may be our undoing. Unfortunately, the economy is not run by logic and reason. There is no computer, no committee, or great mind guiding our markets. Instead, the blind are leading the blind. The Federal Reserve Board has its limits. There may come a day, sooner than many of us would like, when logic and reason finally opens the eyes of investors, leaving fear and greed to trigger a stampede to safety.

America will endure, but the lifestyle to which we are accustomed may not. That is why you need to be aware of what can happen, especially some of the more plausible financial dangers, and do all you can to prepare for them.

So, what is there to fear?

03:00

When Cometh "The End"?

"Wolf!"

Hear it enough times without seeing the dreaded beast, the old fable goes, and soon you just ignore anyone and anything that smacks of false prophecy.

Even investment guru Warren Buffett, one of the richest men in the world, admitted to "crying wolf" too many times.[7] But sooner or later, the worst forecaster is going to blunder on to something.

And yet there is an intriguing, if not distressing, convergence of contrasting viewpoints concerning the future of our economy. It brings to mind the 1984 movie "Ghostbusters," where the heroes are required to battle the "enormous mystical convergence."[8]

We can laugh at the comedy. But who's to say our economy is not bringing together all the ingredients for a disturbance that comes once every few hundred years? The sky may be clear now, but a once-in-a-century storm could be in the making. The last time something like this occurred it was called a depression.

Many are poised for financial disaster because they believe in an end-of-the-world event. Smug self-proclaimed realists (and that probably means each of us -- in a way, we all think we are right) smirk at religious fundamentalists and their fatalistic belief of impending doom. Yet three of the world's largest religions, Christianity, Islam, and Judaism, with more than 53% of the world's population, or nearly three billion people[9], all have the same basic tenet that some day there will be a cataclysmic end to the world. Christians, who make up the largest faith, believe no one knows when the end will come[10], but millions feel it is inevitable and may happen in the near future.

Conspiracy theorists, on the other hand, many of them part of those same religionists with an extremely negative outlook on life, have what they call "proof" that there is a small group of Swiss bankers who pull all the financial strings of the world's money bags. Rather than only believe in canonized prophecies, these theorists would prefer to believe there is some grand Market Manipulation going on in Zurich.

Even those who do not consider themselves religious worry global warming may change the world as we know it. Just look at all the end–of-the-world movies that have hit the big screens in the past decade.

Unfortunately, as proven by the horrific happenings of September 11, 2001, some who fall within the cultist category of terrorists feel it is their destiny to bring on the destruction of the "evil empires" of the world.

While they are perhaps the most evil of all, their actions definitely have an effect on the financial markets. There are many other factors that affect the economy, but history shows few events provide more uncertainty than this kind of terrorism.

What could cause another great crash to happen?

Historically, astonishing and troublesome news reports such as Pearl Harbor, the Korean War, Sputnik, the Cuban Missile Crisis, or 9/11 have caused the stock market to drop. But within a short period of time the market usually rebounded. What is valuable to analysts is not the knee-jerk emotional plummet of the indexes but the mid-term reaction months after the report. Healthy markets were able to continue on their upward climb, while breaking stories bearing bad news encouraged an already struggling economy to falter.

The next financial downturn might be influenced by a nation-wide panic brought on by terrorists, but it is more likely any future depression will be the result of cold, hard economic reality.

Ultimately sound minds need to stop and review the serious nature of the economic facts that have been broiling for years. How often do you get such diverse groups as long-term academic historians, macro and micro economists, fiscal analysts, and investment theorists to all independently agree?

Their agreement is almost universal: something has got to give!

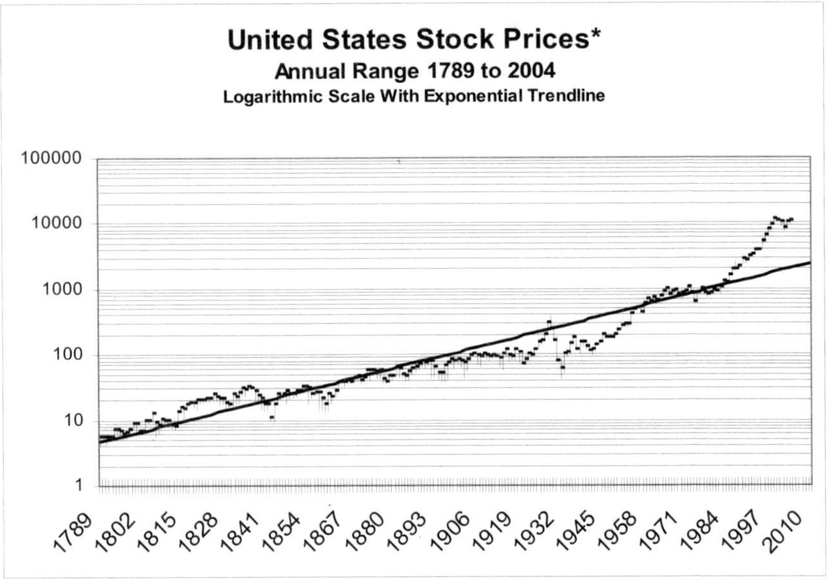

INDEX PAST PERFORMANCE IS NOT INDICATIVE OF FUTURE RESULTS
The United States Stock Prices Chart is a composite of the Dow Jones Industrial Average from 1920 to 2004, Cowles Commission provided by Yale University, 1880-1920, and the Foundation for the Study of Cycles, 1789 to 1880.

Breathe-In, Breathe-Out, Breathe-In....

No doubt you noticed the chart.[11]

That is one long upward trend. Now, look closely at the dates. The United States stock market from 1789 to the early 2000s has made a dramatic climb.

What investor wouldn't like to see their portfolio make a lot of money all the time? When the stock market moves downward good investment advisers remind their clients it is normal and in their best interest to have a breather every so often. This movement is required, just as it is with any living person. If all you did was breathe in you would fall over in a dead faint. You have to breathe out every time you take a breath.

Any healthy economy needs the same opportunity to pull back to stay alive.

To illustrate, the following chart displays the typical course of a short-term economic business cycle over the real life drama of the stock market. The bottom line represents the long term growth trend. The cycle includes the "peaks" of expansion (the high points) and the "troughs" of contraction, also known as a recession (the low points).

The Economic Cycle From Peak to Trough
(Dow Jones Average)

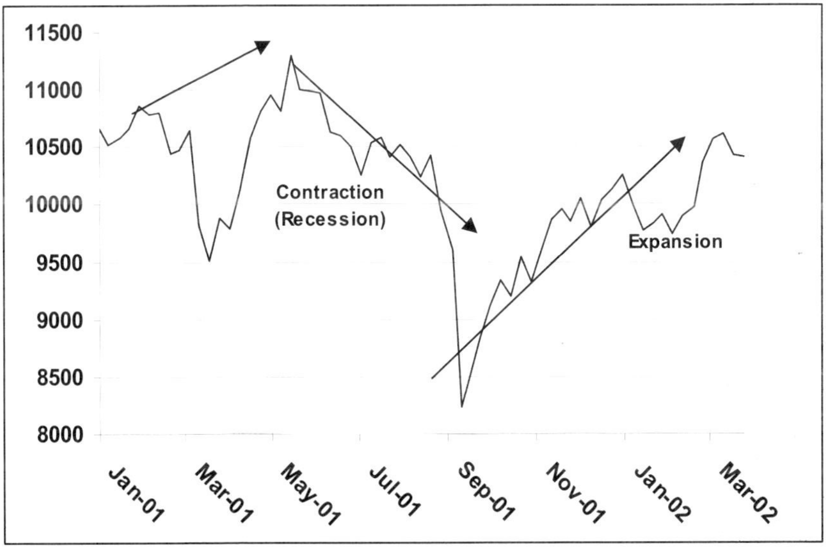

INDEX PAST PERFORMANCE IS NOT INDICATIVE OF FUTURE RESULTS.

Many financial advisors say there is no industry accepted method to tell when the market will go down. So they say you might as well stay invested through the good, the bad, and the downright ugly.

But begging to differ, as some analysts review the world's long-term economy over the last few hundred years and how it relates to today's stock market, certain theories have emerged all based on trying to second guess what will happen in the future.

Elliott-Wave theorists see a trend on both the long-term and short-term graphs. Dating back to the dark ages, investors who follow the Wave theories believe that the charts speak for themselves. Elliotticians, as they are called, believe they can forecast the outcome of the stock market based solely on historical trends.

The Elliott-Wave theory suggests that the stock market moves in the same methodical motion the ocean does. The market tide ebbs and flows in major movements or "super-cycles" in periods of hundreds of years. Then there are regular "waves" coming and going, such as the ten year period between the peaks of 1973 and 1983, with many smaller waves, called "subwaves," during the larger movement of the market.

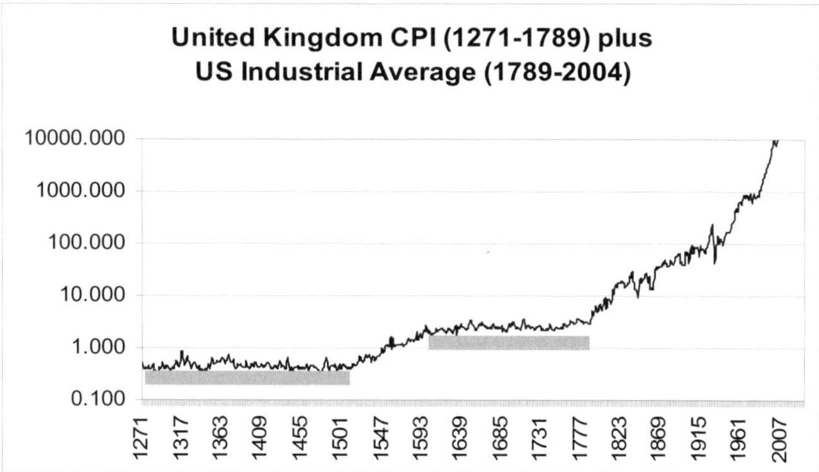

INDEX PAST PERFORMANCE IS NOT INDICATIVE OF FUTURE RESULTS.

The frequency of these cycles and waves is believed to be as dependable as nature. Still, the theorists attempt to be practical. The Elliott-Wave theory encourages investors to be flexible and to "allow for immense diversity of specific outcome, [because] the market is no exception. All that can be said about ratio analysis at this point is that comparing the price lengths of waves frequently confirms, often with pinpoint accuracy, the applicability to the stock market…."[12]

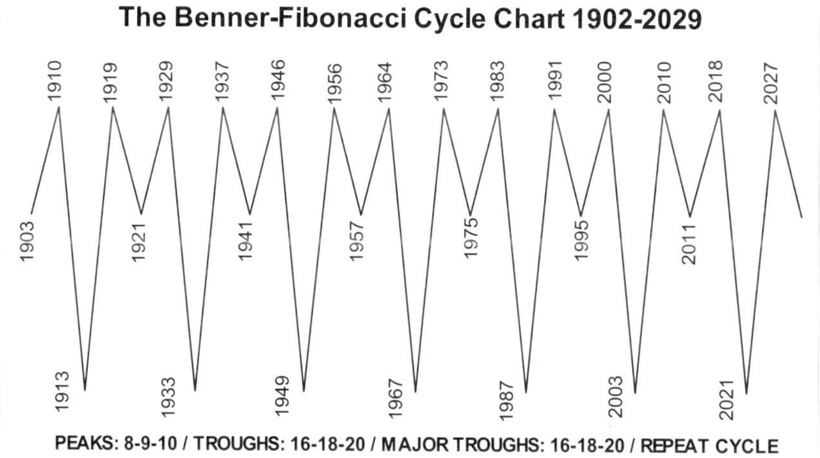

INDEX PAST PERFORMANCE IS NOT INDICATIVE OF FUTURE RESULTS.

Wave theorists use the Benner-Fibonacci Cycle, reformulated in the Bank Credit Analyst in 1967, as a general guide to forecast future moves in the market. The formula suggests market waves emerge in a consistent pattern with peaks, troughs, and major troughs. Those who follow this theory determined the first major trough of the new millennium would come in 2003. Sure enough, the Dow Jones Industrial Average dropped to a low of 7177 in October 2002 and nearly repeated the dip to 7397 in March 2003.

While this Cycle is not an exact science, it does reasonably reflect past movements in the market, give or take a year. Looking into the future, investors using the Benner-Fibonacci Cycle forecast the stock market to peak in 2010 with a minor trough in 2011. The next peak would be in 2018 with a major trough in 2021.

Similar market expectations have been derived using other economic theories. Whether you use the ***Random-Walk Theory*** which has evolved out of the ***Efficient-Markets Theory***, or any other idea, the basic concept is that equilibrium must exist in any healthy market.

At its fundamental level, equilibrium in the stock market, or the Random-Walk Theory, is not difficult to understand. Imagine for a moment that you begin a random walk from your home in the valley and head towards the hills. Occasionally as you stop and look back you are elated as you enjoy the beautiful vistas. Your hike is thrilling as you continue to head towards the highest point where you are finally able to sit for a moment and view the scene below. You feel a sense of satisfaction and completion. However after time, as with any journey, you must continue on with your trek. Even if you continue traveling in the same direction your random walk will take you back down the other side of the mountain until you reach the next valley.

Elliotticians, like good naturalists, will point out the equilibrium concept within their own theory. As the ocean's tide flows in and out the waves never go on forever. In due course there is a point where gravity takes over and pulls everything back to normalcy.

Meanwhile, most economists, using various theories and mathematical ratios, say a day of economic reckoning is coming. They can not universally agree where the top of the mountain is, they just know it must be up there, somewhere in the clouds.

Arriving at the same conclusion through different methods, academics confirm the expected drop. Two respected economists from Yale University, John Campbell and Robert Shiller, also do not have an optimistic outlook for the long-term economy.

Their research reviewed forecasting methods using valuation variables such as the dividend-price and the price-smoothed-earnings ratios. They state, "These ratios are not forecasting variables that were discovered yesterday.... [Rather they have] been continually discussed over the last century."[13]

This research team concludes their report with more questions than answers. Campbell and Shiller ask whether the ratios used in the past are reliable. Their conclusion is a sobering one:

"While we do not expect a complete return to traditional valuation levels, we still interpret the broad variety of evidence is suggesting a poor long-term outlook for the stock market."[14]

But Wait! There's More!

Bad news often is reminiscent of the knife infomercials where there is always a promise of something more. In this case it is doom and gloom.

Reviewing the "facts," or at least the projections which are based on facts, the short to mid-term forecasts appear positive, but the long-term outlook is dismal.

Demographic economist Harry S. Dent has been researching the ever-changing face of America. He bases his educated guess on the spending habits of the population as it moves through its life cycles. He was among the first economists and trend watchers who stated the obvious: certain companies will be better long-term investments as Americans grow older, such as drug companies. Looking back we may call it "obvious," but it took analysts like Dent to point it out.

Lifecycle researchers have closely watched Americans as they age, get married, raise a family, buy a home, pay for their college loans, and prepare for retirement. These cycles have all come in very predictable patterns. Early in the 1990s, Mr. Dent predicted the Dow Jones Industrial Average would reach 10,000 or higher by the year 2000. In that year the market stood at only 2,500. He was right on target as the market hit more than 11,900 by 2000! What is important to remember is that this was an internal growth rate of 16%. Now, using that same formula, Dent and other forecasters are predicting that the market will reach a range as high as 30,000 by the year 2009.[15]

Consider the Dow Channel chart from 1982 to 2010, which is anchored by the two-decade-long Internet and computer technology boom. Assuming the pattern continues, the trend appears headed for a range between 20,000 and 40,000 by 2010. This stock market level is not unrealistic, especially if Social Security accounts are privatized and add to the buying frenzy.

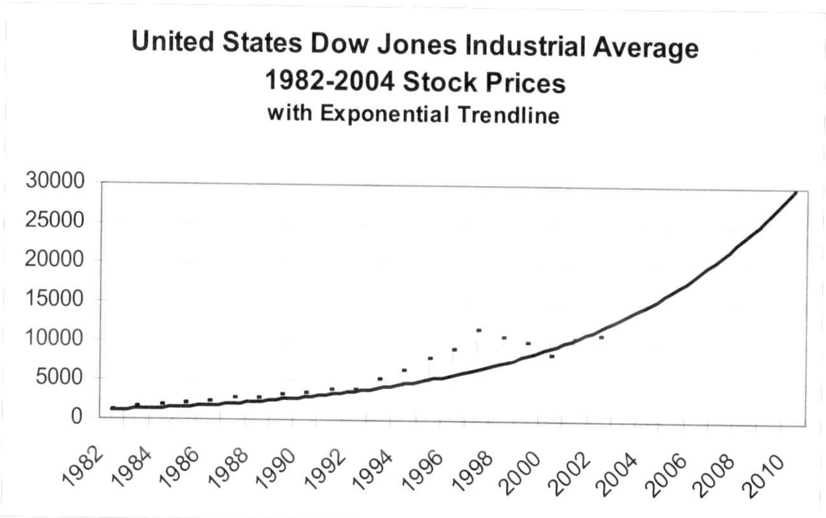

INDEX PAST PERFORMANCE IS NOT INDICATIVE OF FUTURE RESULTS.

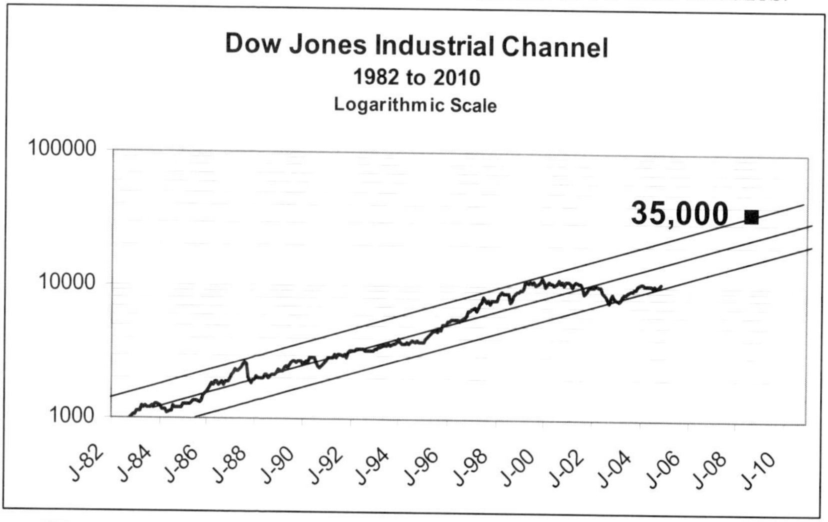

INDEX PAST PERFORMANCE IS NOT INDICATIVE OF FUTURE RESULTS.

If the trend continues, most investors will be very pleased as the market more than doubles in five years. However, the economy can be derailed by any number of external events.

What matters is not the potential level of the market, but the fact that forecasters warn there is a definite limit to the market's growth. Economists use the Dow Jones 10-year Decennial Pattern (ten decade long averages of the past 100 years) to predict the market will hit a ceiling and then take a significant drop.

When analyzing this information, researcher Ned Davis stresses "Trend is more important than level."[16] In other words, the amount is not as important as the direction of the market. Using demographic trends and economic cycles, analysts predict a temporary drop in the market in 2006 to 2007. Then, after a brief interlude, the market will continue its upward climb. Dent says, "Two moderate cycles [will] hit in 2010 alone with strong downward demographic trends after mid-2009. Hence we feel it is extremely likely that we will see a top by late 2009 and a strong downturn in 2010." A growing number of economists agree that a major bear market will begin around 2009 or 2010 and last through 2020 to 2022.[17]

Less than a month after the September 11th terrorist attack on America, 1500 stockbrokers and investment advisors from around the country attended a national conference with the desire to glean as much information as possible to help their clients. Standing before the concerned group, Dr. Robert Goodman described the positive scenario of the first decade of the 21st-century, but then detailed how the second decade could be a very challenging time.

Dr. Goodman's message echoed that of the others. Through 2010 the economy is prepared to return to its growth patterns of the 1990s, but thereafter, it may be a very difficult time for investors.[18]

The market is expected to rise but there are enough potential roadblocks that could derail the economy sooner.

Will it happen? Who knows?

The warning voice has been sounded for years. Economists and analysts are concerned trends could lead to a Depression that might last for more than a decade, possibly from 2010 to 2022, making the Great Depression of the 1930s seem mild in comparison.

Will History Repeat Itself?

Consider the record: starting in August 1929, at 380 points, the Dow Jones Industrial Average dropped more than 50% by October 1930. It fell more than 50% again by September 1931. By June 1932 the market finished its crash by plummeting again more than 50%, bottoming out at 42 points.

Turn back to page 20 and look at the United States Stock Prices chart from 1789 to 2004 and the exponential trend line. Assuming forecasters are correct, the Dow Jones average could reach 20,000 or more by 2010. But that is far above the historical trend line. *If* "trend is more important than level," and *if* there is something that stimulates a downward movement, then, just like the 1929 to 1932 crash, the market *could* return to the trend line by dropping 50%

three times: once from 20,000 to 10,000, again declining 50% to 5,000, and finally, falling 50% to 2,500, right where the trend line says we should be.

Truly, the "INDEX PAST PERFORMANCE IS NOT INDICATIVE OF FUTURE RESULTS." This statement usually is designed to discourage bullishly optimistic expectations of the short term growth in the market. It also applies to overly negative talk. We need to be cautious with trend lines. Just because people in the 1800s died at 50 years of age and now we are living to 100, does that mean that by the end of the next few centuries we will live to 200 or 400 years of age because of the "trend"? It is impossible to imagine! At the same time, market averages have nothing to do with our finite life spans. Yet the economy has its limits. Usually the only way the chart continues to move upward after "market saturation" is due to inflation.

Statistics, analytical research, economics, and many other scientific methods can be used to prove any point of view. However, even the ill-informed and the uninformed are able to see the writing on the wall. All that is needed is a reporter to point out the glaring facts.

And the most glaring "fact" of all is the need to be ready.

04:00

The Aging of America and The Retirement Crisis

Ask any hopeful college student to describe their expectations for retirement. Most likely they will say their goal is to be financially secure by the time they are 55. That's when they plan on having the money to do what they want. But that dream for the more realistic graduate might be a hope of the past.

The dream of retirement might also be crushed for many of the 200-million working Americans looking forward to the time they can sit back and enjoy the good life.

The reason their future plans may be ruined is due to the millions of people who will be retiring during the first three decades of the 21st Century. The repercussion of their removal from employment will be felt for years.

There are other concerns that may add to the crisis. Long-term economic cycles are expected to bring a period of time when the economy retracts. Then the pendulum of changing power in our government may result in increased taxes, soaring government debt or decreased benefits, decreased economic expansion, and the possibility of high inflation. With these factors working against the economy, past decisions by Congress to fill the public's demand for guaranteed bank accounts may actually add to the instability of the system. Finally, if America shows any sign of internal weakness the political, economic, and social uncertainties of the world will escalate and compound the problem.

When presented with these trials some commentators suggest that immigration will replace the outflow of retirees and will fix the problem. But all the ideas that have been presented to this date may not be enough.

In the long run, the grand ocean liner America should not sink, but enough damage can be caused that will make life barely tolerable for many, and downright miserable for those who did not listen to the warning.

Each of these issues, acting independently, may, like a long row of dominos, start a chain reaction that could present a very bleak picture for the future. Whatever happens, provident living teaches the need to be aware of the potential challenges that lie ahead, and prepare like they are a real threat.

Fed Chairman Alan Greenspan has warned for years about our uncertain future. He has suggested the years around 2012 could be a pivotal time in the world.[19] He prefers to use the word "opaque" when describing what might happen in the second decade. But the years beginning 2009 to 2012 will bring a real economic time bomb caused by the aging of America's workplace and the irrational deficit spending of the United States Congress.

To quote Mr. Greenspan and the CBS News, "The benefits already promised have created a situation where Congress has promised a level of spending 'in excess of our capability to finance it.... When we get into the period beyond 2010, 2011, 2012, we are running into potentially serious problems.'"[20]

No longer pulling any punches, in August, 2004, the Fed Chairman, bluntly described the future of America: "The aging of the population in the United States will significantly affect our fiscal situation."[21]

The Baby "Busters"

In the 1930s, migrant workers moved from job to job in their beat up old jalopies, often with a sign proclaiming their destination, listing the state or city followed by the words "or bust." They expected to either make it or break down. Their great grandchildren, in the early decades of the 2000s, may well coin the phrase "Retirement or Bust!" for good reason. There is the chance some retirees will be greeted with a world very different than the one they were expecting.

Consider the following analysis. In the year 2005 there were more than 77 million "Baby Boomers," those people born between 1946 and 1964. By the time they reach retirement the number will probably dwindle to 57.8 million. (The decrease in numbers will occur because death will catch up with many in their 70s.)

It is unsettling that the United States Census Department, projects by the year 2030 there will be nearly twice as many retirees as 25 years earlier!

Some analysts suggest the retiring Baby Boomers will begin spending like never before pushing the market upward. They say the retirees will cash out their retirement accounts for their long awaited leisure and travel plans.

Other forecasters disagree and warn the result will not be so optimistic because the loss of 77 million workers will deplete the labor market and drive up salaries for a small supply of qualified replacements. Higher salaries will probably mean higher inflation. In addition, some demographers say the Baby Boomers may become cautious,[22] putting their spending plans on the back burner so their finances will last throughout the rest of their longer-than-originally-expected lives.

Compared to 2005, the U.S. Census[23] projections show:

> By 2020: 48% more retirees. 27% less workers paying taxes to sustain each retiree
>
> By 2030: 93% more retirees. 43% less workers paying taxes to sustain each retiree

By 2050: There will be almost 20 million people older than 85, nearly ***four*** times more than in 2005.

The Numbers Tell it All

In 2005 there were 5.3 people capable of working (16 to 64 years old) per each person in the 65+ group. By 2020 that number will drop to 3.8 and ten years later the number will plummet to 3.0.

Comparing the number of retirees with the taxpayers who have reached their career goals, the more mature group of employees normally considered as "head of households" (ages 30 to 64), by 2030, the ratio drops to only 2.0 workers for each retired person.

Toss in the children, under 16, who are not working, and the stark reality is that half the income from each person working in 2030 will pay for the support, taxes, and other expenses for an extra person, whether or not they are a part of their family. This category has been aptly termed the "Total Dependency Ratio" by the United Nations in their review of aging.[24]

By 2030, grey hair (or colored hair or bald heads) will be much more common as one out of five people will be over 64. The number of people living past 100 will increase 300%! Health will improve, longevity of life will increase, but there is a big question mark when it comes to whether lifestyle will improve.

The results may be astonishing.

Retirement in the first half of the century will be like everyone going to the amusement park at once. It was a great idea when it was planned. But the moment the retirees get there, they will realize that every one else had the same idea. By the end of the day, it will no longer be fun. Everybody will be grumpy and upset after waiting in long lines and finding the stay will not be as enjoyable as hoped.

When it comes to retirement planning, the retirees will not have many choices. There will come a time when the aging process will get in the way of effectiveness at work and they will be required to quit, whether or not they have enough money saved up for their care.

The economy can only react in one of three ways. The national financial system will go up, sideways, or down. According to some experts the probable result for the stock market will be to head back down to its long term trend line, a potential drop of 75% to 90%. It happened in 1929 to 1932. This time the retirees could be the catalyst.

The World Around US

This real time bomb has not singled out the United States. It is an unfixable predicament as many nations face a drastically declining population base. This old age explosion will change everything in the world wide economy: resource allocation, consumption, investment patterns, housing, fashion, entertainment and many other industries.

In April 2002, the United Nations convened the "Second World Assembly on Ageing". The resulting

Executive Summary is so gloomy that it deserves to be quoted as follows: (the highlighting is ours, and the U.N. English spells it "Ageing")

1. **Population Ageing Is Unprecedented**, without parallel in the history of humanity. Increases in the proportions of older persons (60 years or older) are being accompanied by declines in the proportions of the young (under age 15). By 2050, the number of older persons in the world will exceed the number of young for the first time in history. Moreover, by 1998 this historic reversal in relative proportions of young and old had already taken place in the more developed regions.

2. **Population Ageing Is Pervasive**, a global phenomenon affecting every man, woman and child. The steady increase of older age groups in national populations, both in absolute numbers and in relation to the working-age population, has a direct bearing on the intergenerational and intra-generational equity and solidarity that are the foundations of society.

3. **Population Ageing Is Profound**, having major consequences and implications for all facets of human life. In the economic area, population ageing will have an impact on economic growth, savings, investment and consumption, labour markets, pensions, taxation and intergenerational transfers. In the social sphere, population ageing affects health and health care,

family composition and living arrangements, housing and migration. In the political arena, population ageing can influence voting patterns and representation.

4. **Population Ageing Is Enduring**. During the twentieth century the proportion of older persons continued to rise, and this trend is expected to continue into the twenty-first century. For example, the proportion of older persons was 8 per cent in 1950 and 10 per cent in 2000, and is projected to reach 21 per cent in 2050.[25]

The underlying international message: the world will be "transformed," and these unprecedented changes will not be reversed.

At one time it was popular to worry about a population explosion. Although some countries, such as India, will continue to endure huge birthrates, in many countries a population implosion is occurring. One report states that Eastern Europe, including Russia, will see a contraction of 25% by the year 2050, or in other words, 82 million people will not be replaced. "Overall Europe is expected to lose 17% of its population by mid-century, some 124 million people. That is an extraordinary change whose impacts will be deep, long lasting and profound."[26]

Another demographic disaster is unfolding on the other side of the world. Since the 1990s, Japan has felt the aging crisis perhaps more acutely than most other countries as its economy has taken a dramatic plunge. There was a time when management gurus stressed the importance of businesses becoming "more Japanese." Now, it appears that Japan may never return to its once prominent position in the world economy. According to national and international statisticians, Japan is becoming smaller day by day. This is due to declining fertility rates, a refusal to allow immigration because of the desire to avoid genetic shift, and the unavoidable fact that the Japanese people, as a whole, are getting older. The end result may be nothing more than a picture of the things to come for the leading nations of the world. Japan is moving away from consumerism and may soon become one of the world's largest retirement centers![27]

Japanese Population Pyramids
1950/2000/2050 (projected)

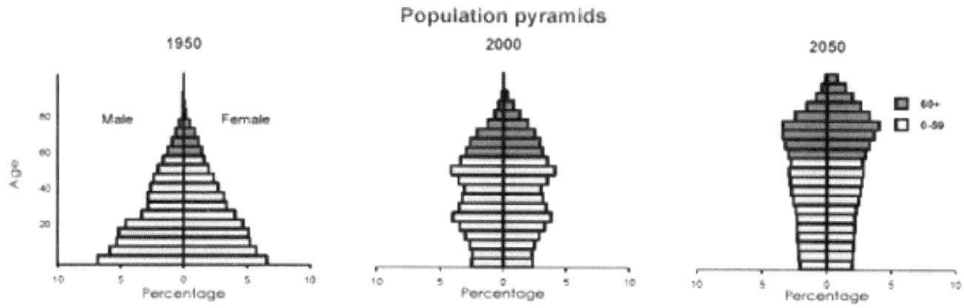

Source: UN Report: World Population Ageing, 1950-2050

In 1950, Japan's population, shown in the above graph from the youngest to the oldest, created a very healthy pyramid with a firm foundation. Since that time declining fertility rates and increasing longevity have resulted in a top-heavy graph. By 2050 the graph shows a tiny foundation where the feeble elderly will dominate.

The United Nations identified the need to care for increasing numbers of elderly as the "Potential Support Ratio". It compares the number of people in the work force aged 15-64 to every person aged 65 and older. This "Potential Support" grouping was compiled to identify those who will be available to work as caretakers. In Japan, the ratio in 1950 was 12.1; by 2000 it fell to 4.0; by 2025, it will drop another 50% to 2.0 and by 2050 it is projected to decline to 1.4, one of the lowest in the world.[28]

The United States will not be not far behind Japan, with a ratio of 2.9 people available to care for every one elder in 2050. Analysts around the world recognize one of the greatest problems facing economies such as the United States is the need to find and keep qualified caretakers. This has never been a simple process for progressive, skilled, and highly paid economies because few workers are patient enough to be underpaid and underappreciated.

A Drastic Lifestyle Change

The population explosion of retiring Baby Boomers over a relatively short period of time – 18 years – may create a dramatic change in America's standard of living. The huge influx of elderly will result in a health care and long-term-care industry ready to burst.

The economy will be affected in a number of ways. The government is expecting worker productivity to fall, especially for women in their fifties and sixties, who are the normal caretakers of the elderly. This will further drain the financial system as this significant portion of the workplace will be forced to quit, or to work part time in order to care for their older relatives. This comes at an inopportune time when they are trying to save for their own retirement benefits, adjust to the loss of a family member, or put their child through college all the while living with a reduced income.[29]

Researchers who study the aging of America have painted a grim picture of how our standard of living will be affected by the increased number of elderly. Demographers say the ratio of elderly to their children was one in three back in 1950. One hundred years later, in 2050, there will be 29 people over the age of 65 for each person between the ages of 50 and 65![30]

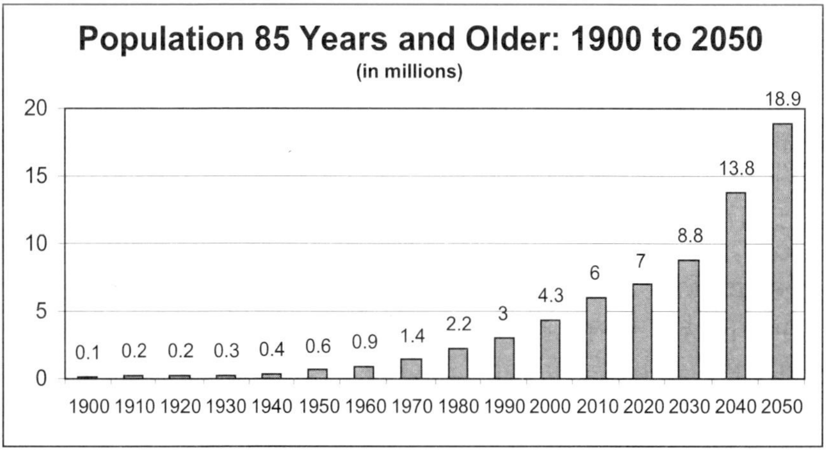

Source: U.S. Bureau of the Census[31]

By the time this group of retirees reach old age (over 85), one in five people will be retired. This means that a significant percentage of the nation's consumers will have a completely different spending mindset. Old buying habits will be replaced by cautious pessimism. Fear will play an ever increasing role as the new elderly come to the realization that their accounts must have enough money to last for the next 30 years. Retirees will not immediately stop spending, but industries will be affected by the change in spending habits when they start to cut back.

Demographic economist Harry Dent, describing the coming tidal wave of older Americans, pointed out the spending trends of people from the 1970s into the 2000s. The stock market did very well for certain companies that marketed towards the Boomer age group. For example, in the 70s, Kimberly-Clark had a run on its stock while the Pampers brand diaper was very popular with the new disposable get-it-done-now age group of consumers. As they grew older and more financially secure, their needs and tastes changed. Companies that provided feel-good products for the middle to upper class excelled. Examples of future industries which will take care of the needs of the millions of retirees will be tourism and health-care, if there is any money left.

The advancement of medical technology just might backfire on the fun-loving, go-anywhere, do-anything-they-can-afford Baby Boomers. Demographic analysts and statisticians are now required to factor in the increased duration of chronic illness and the need for long-term care for the elderly.

The health-care industry, which includes pharmaceuticals, may not have an unfettered future. The more expensive it becomes for insurance companies to subsidize the aging population and their every medical whim, the more likely insurance costs will escalate out of reach of the common person. It may be only a matter of time before the United States government will be forced to follow the path of many other countries to socialized medicine.

In addition to the emotional stress felt by millions of older people trying to prolong life, their children, grand-children, and extended family will also feel the strain of caring for their frail loved ones.

Long-term care is going to get more expensive for taxpayers. Another factor that will play a considerable role in our future is the lifestyle of 20 million of these retirees. The Census Department statistics reveal 26% of the Baby Boomers did not have children.[32] Leaders are anticipating a huge number of elderly expecting to be institutionalized. Statistics show that a large number of older people will be women with no family to care for them.

Jobs Needing the Patience of Job

In the first fifty years of this century, many industries will be affected in one way or another by the aging of America. An evolution will occur in the way industries carry on their business practices, including research and development, recruiting, marketing, and distribution.

For example, one trade that will need a healthy influx of employees is the financial services industry. However recruiters and consultants already are worried there will be a drought of qualified financial advisers. In 2010, there will be 10 million more jobs than workers to fill them, according to an analysis of Department of Labor statistics.[33]

So, what jobs will be needed to take care of the growing retirement community? One writer, attempting to be upbeat, looks at the positive, and suggests that small businesses will thrive, assuming all retirees will be "richer," "healthier," and "independent". Home-based jobs such as fitness organizations, adult day care, geriatric care management, hospice care, elder relocation, chauffeuring, and elder companion, are just some of the business ideas available to care for an older population.[34] However, unless there is a major shift in what people are willing to pay for a service, these positions will not provide the income required to develop careers or replace missing taxes from the depleted government accounts.

Currently, professional caregivers are usually paid up to two times minimum wage. However, in the future there will be a migration of lower paid workers to the higher paying jobs left over from the retiring Baby Boomers. If the pay structure stays the same for the caregivers, some studies show there will be a dramatic decline in the number of caregivers per older person. There will be an additional drain on all of society as the ratio of elderly people to homecare workers will increase from seven to one in the year 2000 to twenty-four to one in 2050! Study after study says the system as we know it today will become unaffordable in the next ten years.[35]

The future lifestyle of the elderly will change in the next 50 years as more retirees will be pushed into poverty. Because older men are normally married and die sooner, the majority of elderly women will be single and live alone. As the average lifespan increases in the United States, the largest majority of people living past 85 will be women, and most will be institutionalized at the expense of the government.[36] Most women, especially those who were in the workforce, never imagined that they would need to save enough to last more than 20 years. An increasing number of caregivers will be needed to assist the old and frail.

Even hard-to-handle cases will increase in frequency. By 2050, scientists in one study predict that the number of people with Alzheimer's disease will increase by more than 300% from 4.5 million to 13.2 million.[37] Individual states which attract retirees, such as Florida and Arizona, will feel the budget crunch even more as state health departments scramble to take care of the needy.

Current statistics from the Congressional Budget Office (CBO) project nearly one of every two retirees will need some long-term care assistance in a nursing home during their life.[38] But the averages do not take into account the months or years an elderly person may struggle to care for their own needs.

Few people who have cared for the feeble elderly will describe it as “easy”. It is a time-consuming and emotion-draining task that can last two to five years or more. And the more the medical industry is able to prolong life, the more long-term assistance will be needed. Helping a 120 pound (or more) adult is not the same as caring for and watching a twenty pound toddler. Lifting their dead weight off the floor or out of bed; steadying their struggling body as they try to make it to the shower or wheelchair; providing proper dosages of medication; ensuring that enough food and liquids are taken to maintain health; graciously lending a listening ear as they struggle to communicate; clothing them, brushing their teeth, combing their hair, changing their diapers, supporting them with the simplest of personal hygiene; the list goes on and on. It takes a special person capable of the physical demands and the emotional requirements to be kind and long-suffering twenty-four hours a day.

Because a large number of the elderly will not have the personal savings ready to pay for long-term care, the Congressional Budget Office estimates that the overall expenditure for long-term care will increase nearly fourfold by 2050 until it becomes a draining factor on the country. By the mid-point of the century, the cost could be nearly a half a trillion dollars a year.[39] While the Government suggests private insurance policies may increase the availability of custodial support for the Baby Boomers, the budget office warns there are a number of risks.[40] These risks include the uncertainty whether the insurance industry will be able to continue to provide service at an affordable price, and the very real potential for the insurers to go bankrupt.

Coming Up Next...

Our future lifestyle changes can be identified by any number of comparisons. Just a few will make the point.

When Franklin D. Roosevelt approved the Social Security system in 1935, the fabric of society was very different as there were 42 workers for each retired person who was expected to only live to 65 years of age! Compare the following:

	1937	2005	2030
Workers Compared to One Retiree (Eligible workers in 2005 and 2030)	12	5.28	2
Life Expectancy (years)	65	77	81
Social Security Tax Rate	2%	12.4%	16.6% (Expected)

U.S. Census Bureau and Social Security Administration

The aging of America's Baby Boomers will completely overhaul our understanding and expectation of retirement. It is a problem that can be likened to a huge iceberg. The ocean liner America is inching closer to the icy tip, but lurking beneath is the unseen danger that could rip a gaping hole in the fragile underside of our retirement sightseeing trip.

Dr. Ken Dychtwald suggests that the Baby Boomers are the do-it-yourself spenders who gave birth to companies like Home Depot, but few of these educated retirees are emotionally and financially prepared for the future.[41] This will be a time where traditional pension plans will play an increasingly minor role and the invest-yourselfers, many of whom are too proud to ask for professional help, may be left on their own to stretch their savings out as long as they can.

Demographers, in 2005, suggest a third of retirees will be well-to-do and another third will be comfortable but wish they had more. But they may not have looked at the big financial picture which foreshadows a struggling economy and a potential loss of value in the retirees' portfolios.

The final third of the Baby Boomers generation, Dr. Dychtwald warns, is “at the bottom, about 25 million Boomers who have less than $1000 in net lifetime assets.”[42] Taxpayers will likely be required to step forward to meet the health-care and long-term-care needs of this sizable group of people. Increased taxes and inflation, the result of this huge drain on the economy, could potentially cause the market to be dragged into a spiraling dive.

This time there may be no safety net as the federal government will have huge troubles of its own with privatized Social Security and the Medicare crisis.

I Worked For It! I Deserve It!

The vast majority of workers, when they reach 65, or 67 for younger Boomers, will readily put out their hand and ask for, or rather, demand their just reward. Their Social Security check has become an expected old age benefit. Their pensions, saved for years, better be solvent and ready to support the expected lifestyle.

After working 50 years, looking forward to retiring from the daily grind, how many retirees will graciously offer their paycheck to someone else? Who will cheerfully accept that all the money they put aside into Social Security and their retirement funds actually went to another person?

Few people are ready to be so charitable. However, they may not have a choice. Many of the soon-to-be-elderly may be required to continue working well past their expected retirement age if they want to maintain their lifestyle. Eventually old age will catch up with every one, requiring the graying work force to give up work, their income and their precious lifestyle.

Although this is not a new story, people who reach the quitting age will still expect a check. When the money doesn't come as anticipated, they are going to be angry that someone has not come up with an answer to the crisis.

Who wants to be the first to give up their lifestyle, to cut back? And yet analysts are threatening that the impending Social Security explosion will lead to the "greatest financial crisis in America's history."[43]

The people in charge of the Social Security system reported to the U.S. Congress there is a fiscal budget crisis which will lead to the bankruptcy of Medicare Health Insurance by 2019 and Social Security by 2042. The Social Security Trustees report was ominous: "We do not believe the currently projected long run growth rates of Social Security and Medicare are sustainable under current financing arrangements." [44]

One of the think-tanks trying to lead the way for reform, the National Center for Policy Analysis, provided this warning:

> "The looming Social Security crisis is more than a financial crisis; it is a human tragedy that will force us to choose between economic opportunity for our children and retirement security for our parents."[45]

Some of the harshest critics of the system as we know it today, have described Social Security as a pyramid scheme, where the people who come after have paid for the people who came before and there will not be anything left for those left standing. The tragedy in the making may be that old age benefits are nothing but hollow promises for a good life that was a thing of the past.

The reason for the system's demise may have been unwittingly caused by the very lifestyles of the Baby Boomers. Basically, we can either have the "good life" now or later, but not both. It boils down to what mother may have told you: You can have your cake before your vegetables, or after your vegetables, but either way you are going to eat your vegetables.

05:00

Old Age and Taxes and Health, Oh My!

Like characters in some B-Rated monster flick of the 1950s, the masses of law-abiding citizens may someday scream, "Run for your lives!" But after frantically running through the streets, hoping to avoid the dreaded two headed monster of greed and fear, the frightened taxpayers will hopelessly recognize there is nowhere to hide.

In time the realization will set in that the monster was created by the previous generation and nourished by those who are terrorized, and now, someone must face the wrath of the giant's long-anticipated, unleashed fury. The children, now grown up and older, sadly understand that preparation to tame the expected beast should have started years before.

The mournful ending to the story will come when they recognize they could have changed the experiment at any time. They will reluctantly admit someone needs to take control of the situation, and it might as well be them, no matter what the outcome.

Can the sequence of events have a happy ending? The question can have an affirmative answer only if someone takes the helm with a clear vision and the rest of the nation is willing to sacrifice and follow. But that combination seems unlikely.

The Tax Monster

Between the years 2012 and 2031, all 77 million retirees will be transformed. At one moment they were the biggest contributors to our local and national government tax base, but now they have become monstrous consumers asking for their fair share of the trust fund money. Mom and dad, grandpa and grandma were able to retire in leisure. Their pension, coupled with a little social security and free health care made it possible for them to sit back in their motor home and relax.

But the money will not be as readily available to the Baby Boomers. The facts are overwhelmingly stacked against them, and all the hope in the world will not make money out of nothing. The young people entering the labor force will not be able to match the tax contributions of their older counterparts to replenish the old-age pension and health plans.

At one time the Boomers were able to amass a surplus in the Medicare and Social Security accounts. However, when the funds are needed the most, they will not be there. Study after study and analyst after analyst have warned if benefit cuts are not made or higher taxes are not imposed on the retirees, there won't be anything left. Like a dreaded surgery, the longer the patient waits to get started, the less likely the surgery will be a success.

Unfortunately, this topic has been discussed for decades, and each time the familiar phrase similar to the following was used, this time in 1997, "Clearly, Congress must take action soon...."[46] Is "soon," as urged so many years ago, now "too late"?

Anyway, who in their right mind wants to be the politician yoked with such a challenge? If Social Security and Medicare, which comprise the largest governmental department, go bankrupt, and the economy is subsequently hurt, how long will it take other agencies and departments, like the FDIC, Fannie Mae and Freddie Mac, to feel the cancer spread as the enormous budget deficit is uncovered? But one after another they all can come crashing down, causing the instability to spread.

The Government can promise to "protect" or "guarantee," but what will happen to the stock market and the real estate market?

Okay, OKAY!

It is easy to get into a rut, stuck in the mud of pessimism and the pit of despair. It is much more difficult as you're going through the trials to be patient and hopeful and expectant of a bright positive future.

Preparation may be the only way out of the problem.

The Pendulum Trap

The ever-swinging pendulum of taxation and economic expansion takes years, sometimes decades to complete its cycle from one point to another. The last government giveaway began in 2001, the result of a presidential political promise of lower taxes and the desire to give the economy a boost after the 9/11 terrorist attack.

Sure enough, as it has in the past, when the tax cycle has swung as far as it can go, out of necessity, it must retrace its path. It must return to meet the expected demands on the government agencies which dole out billions of dollars in support payments to the masses who do not want to give up what is "theirs".

In the first twenty years of this millennium, economists predict taxes will need to be increased because of (1) the sheer size of the federal budget deficit, (2) the retiring Baby Boomers, and (3) the need to keep up with the expectations that society has placed upon government programs.[47]

Or some group will be required to give up their government benefits, but that does not seem like a realistic option.

The decades leading up to the year 2012 could have painted the economy into a corner with no way out. Economists call it the "liquidity trap". Consider what happened to Japan.

In the early 1980s, Japan was feeling the euphoria of unprecedented expansion. It seemed like the ride would never end. In four years, from 1986 to 1990, everyone thought Japanese stocks were the place to be as the Tokyo Exchange Index increased an astounding 140%, from about 1,200 to nearly 2,900 points. Then came the shocker. During the next twelve years Japan's Index dropped over 70%! Once more the old adage rang true, "What goes up, *must* come down!"

Tokyo Stock Exchange Index[48]

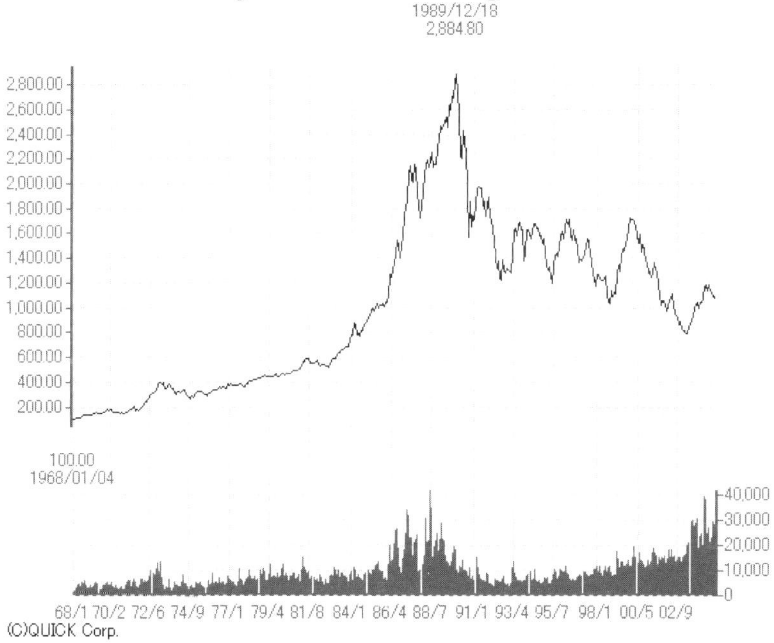

INDEX PAST PERFORMANCE IS NOT INDICATIVE OF FUTURE RESULTS.

The Japanese government watched its economy crash over a relatively short period of time. With the economy nearly lifeless, their financial leaders dropped interest rates almost to zero. At the same time Japan revolutionized the electronic and auto industries, taking a major share of the market, the national monetary control had to take radical measures, even if it meant racking up a huge government deficit just to drive the economy into financial stability.[49] Outside of reaching new markets in far away countries, perhaps Japans' aging population and implosion may be a sign of what could happen with other economies, such as those in the European Union and the United States.

This money trap was last seen in America during the 1930s when the economic decline was so severe drastic measures had to be used to fight the unemployment affecting one out of four families. Even as late as 2003, the United States Federal Reserve Board worried for a moment about the possibility of deflation[50] if the economy required interest rates to be dropped past their 45 year low.

Japan's merchandisers were able to sell to the United States. But who will bail out America? India and China, the next economies expected to boom, have governmental restraints and economic issues to deal with before their consumers will be prepared to buy enough American and Japanese and European exported goods to support the world's self-indulgence.

To Boldly Go Where No One Has Gone Before!

"Uncharted Territory," "Opaque," "Sketchy."[51] These descriptions sound like something from a science fiction movie.

However, this might be the best we can come up with to describe our economic future. It would seem that after decades of brain storming by our most brilliant statisticians, market analysts, and forecasters, someone would be able to give a clearer picture of this future financial puzzle. Or, perhaps, they really do know something and would rather not describe it. Maybe the future will not be pretty and the great thinkers secretly hope someone else will come up with a spectacular idea between now and then to soften the blow.

One study by the mega-accounting firm Ernst and Young, considers the trend that most want to retire early at 62. This staggering report lists an estimated 46 million of the 77 million Baby Boomers will have retired by 2013![52] The report suggests that these Boomers are going to have certain expectations because they have watched for years their parents living the good life. The report states they could get a surprise when they find that all their expectations for leisure and travel may have to be dramatically scaled back. This document is only one of the many which warn the new retirees to be prepared to someday live a life different than planned.[53]

At the same time retirement dreams may be shattered, economists state huge government deficits will loom. News reports[54] say that in the very period of time that tens of millions of retirees will be leaving the job market, the federal deficit will stretch Medicare to bankruptcy and push Social Security there even faster.

MAYDAY! MAYDAY!

For years, the Social Security Administration has been sending out individual reports entitled "Your Social Security Statement" which shows the estimated benefits retirees can expect when they retire. The majority of taxpayers skip the first page which has consistently warned of the department's impending bankruptcy and the need to put as much as possible in other investments. Unfortunately for the retirees living during this period, the dreaded day will soon be here. The Administration Commissioner writes,

> "Social Security can't do it all. You also will need other savings, investments, pensions or retirement accounts to make sure you have enough money to live comfortably when you retire.... [Retirees'] benefits are funded by today's workers and their employers who jointly pay Social Security taxes – just as the money they paid into Social Security was used to pay benefits to those who retired before them.... Without changes... there won't be enough younger people working to pay all of the benefits owed to those who are retiring. At that point there will be enough money to pay only about 73 cents for each dollar of scheduled benefits."[55]

That is over one-fourth, a 27% reduction in benefits!

By then, the tax monster will have grown even larger. The Trustees in charge of the Social Security Administration have been warning of the old-age pension plan's impending demise for years. However, one of their reports warns that even if drastic measures are taken now, it will not be enough!

The following quote comes from the 2004 Trustee's report, almost pleading Congress for drastic action:

> Social Security could be brought into actuarial balance over the next 75 years in various ways, including an immediate increase in payroll taxes of 15 percent or an immediate reduction in benefits of 13 percent (or some combination of the two). To the extent that changes are delayed or phased in gradually, greater adjustments in scheduled benefits and revenues would be required. Ensuring the sustainability of the system beyond 2078 would require even larger changes.[56]

Even if Americans pay large amounts of taxes now and lose out on more benefits for the future, the whole system will still break down!!

Calling it a "crisis" may be understating the obvious. The directors of the federal health insurance and retirement departments are warning the system is sputtering along on fumes and both are heading for a probable break down. Social Security may be bankrupt in the year 2042 and Medicare is expected to go broke as soon as 2019.[57]

As 77 million retirees, one out of five people turn to the government for their paychecks, the potential financial dilemma is enormous. The source of the gaping crack has its origin, not in the wall, or the uneven ceiling line, but in the foundation of the structure, and years of neglect and weathering.

The saddest part of this story is that the Trustees for the Social Security Administration have seen the problem coming for years, but no one has been able to take on the challenge. Who wants to be the bad-guy politician that is required to propose a bill to make Americans pay more for the retirement program they worked so hard to achieve?

Add it up any way you can and the result will be negative.

- More workers retiring
- People living longer
- Health-care expenses going up
- Fewer taxpayers working
- More money going out than coming in
- Government accounts being depleted

To add insult to injury, the Social Security Administration is expecting a downturn in deposits due to the logical increase in retirees. The increase in expenses will begin as early as 2009 with the retirement boom starting just because retirees can and will retire at age 62, with the big peak beginning in 2012.

Privatizing Social Security may be only a part of the answer. America will never know how the concept will work until years after the decision has been made. Allowing young taxpayers the opportunity to invest in the stock market rather than putting their money in the safe haven bond market may provide an immediate quick-fix, but there are potential long-term problems. All the excess cash flowing into the economy will cause a short-term boost, however, when the market takes its regular breather, the drop may be more severe than in the past, losing valuable amounts of retirement savings for some retirees, causing the dwindling number of taxpayers to be responsible for even more support payments.

Social Security Projected Annual Trust Fund Ratios Funds to be Exhausted between 2032 and 2071[58]

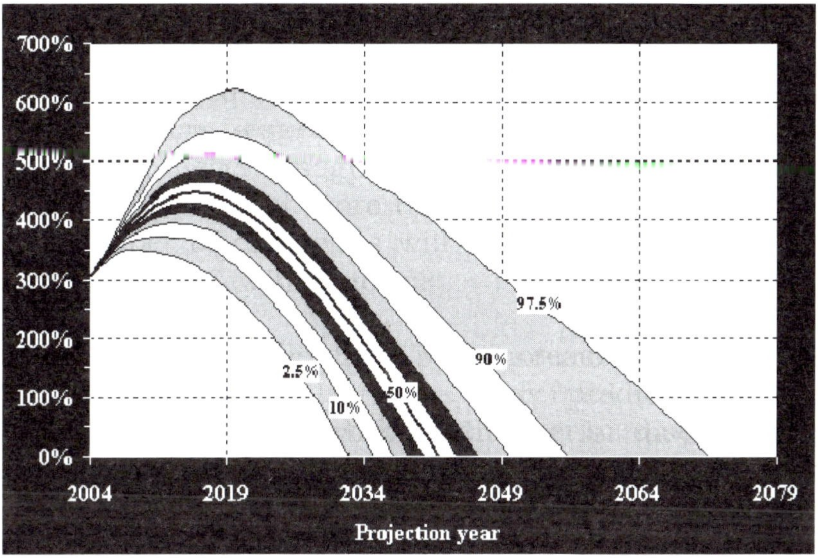

Social Security Administration, 2004

The Rise and Fall of a Free Lunch

Give a toddler their favorite toy, yank it away, and watch what happens.

Give a hungry stray dog a juicy bone and try to grab it away. Watch out for your hand!

Give a retiree a monthly paycheck and free health insurance, after it has been promised for fifty years, and then try to take it away.

Stand back! Get out of the way! Watch out for the tantrum! Don't try to get into this one, because no one wins! When someone feels they deserve what is promised them, they will latch on like a starving bulldog and fight for it all the way.

At the turn of the millennium, Social Security and Medicare were available to everyone. The only requirement was being 62 or 65 years of age. But these expected benefits were not always readily available.

You have to be a trivia buff to be aware of how this entitlement program ever came about in the first place. The current crisis can be traced to the transfer payment entitlement started in Germany in 1889. Chancellor Otto von Bismarck was approached by his government for approval of a payment plan to benefit the civil servant retirees of the German system. Bismarck shrewdly offered a state sponsored saving and investment program which provided security to both the government and the retirees when they reached 65 years of age. The Chancellor knew, in the 1880s, the average European male, once they were able to make it to adulthood, died at 65.8 years of age[59]. In addition, the system set up was a shell game, substituting a "tax on the future earnings of unborn workers for the traditional system of saving and investment."[60]

Workers knew that when they reached a certain age, normally 65, they would have the right to sit back and live out the rest of their life with a consistent income. The program worked like clockwork when there were always more up and coming workers than retirees.

The "entitlement" program swept the globe. The Social Security old-age pension plan made it to America in 1935, and the first check was paid out in 1937.

Medicare, the government supported health insurance plan, arrived in 1965.

The pension system as it evolved in the United States had a few inherent viruses that it picked up from the other transfer payment funding circling the world. These programs all relied on someone else paying for the retirees' lifestyle and health care. The plan did not create any wealth to be transferred to the estate upon the death of the retiree, as it would in a private insurance plan. At least in an insurance policy, the owner would be able to enjoy the benefit of compound interest and if they died early, the excess savings was passed on to their beneficiaries. The other major problem was the change in demographics. The turning of the twenty-first century brought with it too many elderly retirees, not living to only 65, but now living past 85, and not enough young workers to support them all.[61]

In 1983, the U.S. Congress voted to protect Social Security from bankruptcy. But since that time, all the Social Security and Medicare taxes collected from paychecks, which were supposed to be put aside, have actually been legally diverted to pay for other government projects. In addition, the money collected is going straight back into the system, paying for current retirees. This means those who are paying will rely totally on those who come after them. However, when there are not enough young workers to make all the payments the government will have to come up with the rest. But where is it going to come from? The fund now fails the test of short-range financial adequacy as assets drop below the level of the next year's projected expenditures by 2013.[62]

Reviewing the projections, <u>not including Medicare</u>, Social Security will cost Americans a probable 20% and as much as 28% of their paycheck compared to 12.4% at the beginning of the century. Stop and consider the magnitude of this potential tax increase. That is losing another 8% to 16% of your paycheck! That is a 61% to 126% increase in the old age retirement tax!

Social Security Projected Annual Cost Rates[63]

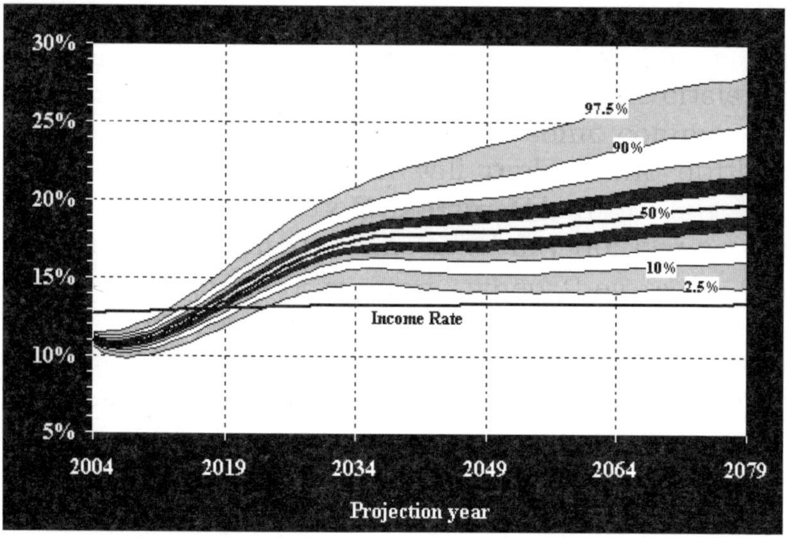

Social Security Administration, 2004

Now, add in the future cost of Medicare Insurance.

Reviewing the following chart, which provides a conservative projection, Medicare Hospital Insurance plus Social Security may someday cost Americans <u>one-third</u> of their paycheck compared to 15.3% at the beginning of the century. Any way you look at it, the taxes supporting pension and old age health insurance, according to the government, will increase 100%. Taxes alone will affect the economy.

Social Security and Medicare Income and Cost Rates
[Percentage Compared to taxable payroll]

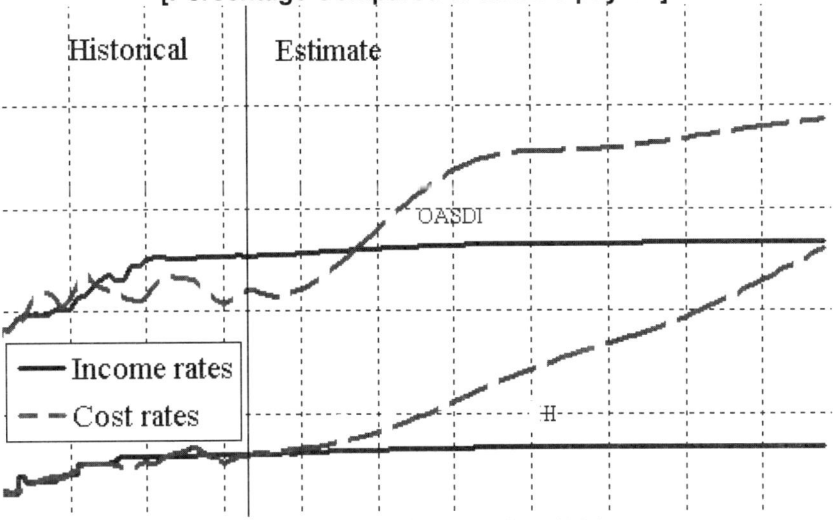

Social Security Administration, 2004

Summarizing the 2004 Social Security Report to Congress, the Trustees said it as concisely as they could:

> It is also evident... that currently projected benefit costs for Medicare and Social Security pose a far more serious long-term financing problem than is generally understood. There is a big increase in the shortfall of dedicated payroll tax and premium income in the 2010 to 2030 period as the "baby-boom" generation reaches retirement age, but this shortfall continues to grow rapidly after that point due to expected faster-than-GDP growth in health care costs and to the increasing life expectancy of beneficiaries. In 2003, the combined annual cost of HI [Medicare

> Hospital Insurance], SMI [Medicare Supplementary Medical Insurance] and OASDI [Old Age and Survivors and Disability Insurance] was about 7 percent of GDP, or two-fifths of total Federal revenues. It is projected to more than double to 15 percent of GDP by 2040 and then to rise further to 20 percent of GDP in 2078, at which time it would exceed total Federal revenues at their historic share of 19 percent of GDP. We do not believe such a long-term rate of growth for the two programs can be sustained. [64]

The Social Security Trustees warn the only way to save the retirement system is to immediately (in 2004) increase the tax to 16.6%. This 4.2% surge in taxes is a growth rate of nearly 34%! Even then there is no guarantee the system will be around after 75 years.[65]

Add the Social Security tax increase to the requirement to increase Medicare to keep pace with the rise in medical services, plus the need to replace the taxes not paid by the retiring Boomers, and the government will have to increase taxes by upwards of ten percent to keep up with expectations. Ten percent taken from the economy either decreases or stagnates the growth of the market especially when the combined income rate of the equity and bond market is less than what is being taken away.

Interpret the preceding report as follows: Americans must expect a major change in income production. If they do not dramatically cut back now, they will not have the funds to enjoy later. Investors should take note that the stock market will suffer either way.

The Options? What Options?

The 1983 Social Security Act did provide some breathing room with a "fail-safe" provision. However, according to analysts, the extra money or "surplus" we were supposed to have as reported by the media, was a mirage.[66] By 2013, the account holding the Social Security fund was expected to have more than $3 Trillion dollars, but the money, for years, will have been used by the government to pay for its other special projects. All that it did was make it possible for Congress to spend more and borrow from the old age trust fund, with the promise that it would pay back at some future date. Once more it was a temporary-fix political move to avoid asking for more money from an already heavily taxed nation.[67]

By 2078, according to the Social Security Trustees, just the cost to keep retirees alive through Medicare Hospital Insurance is projected to have skyrocketed to nearly 14% of the Gross National Product. That is almost 1/7th of everything this country makes.[68]

The budget for Social Security and Medicare at the turn of the century was two-fifths of the federal budget. That is 40% of all the money that is collected goes to old-age insurance and federally funded health insurance. If the trend continues, and there is no sign that it will be different, the Trustees warn ***all*** of the federal budget that was collected in 2004 will go to pay for the elderly in 2078.

The chart on the next page shows how the cost of Medicare Insurance will skyrocket just to keep up with the demands of the elderly.

Medicare Hospital Insurance and Medicare Supplemental Health Insurance (HI+SMI) Compared to Social Security and Disability Insurance (OADI+DI) As a Percentage of GDP[69]

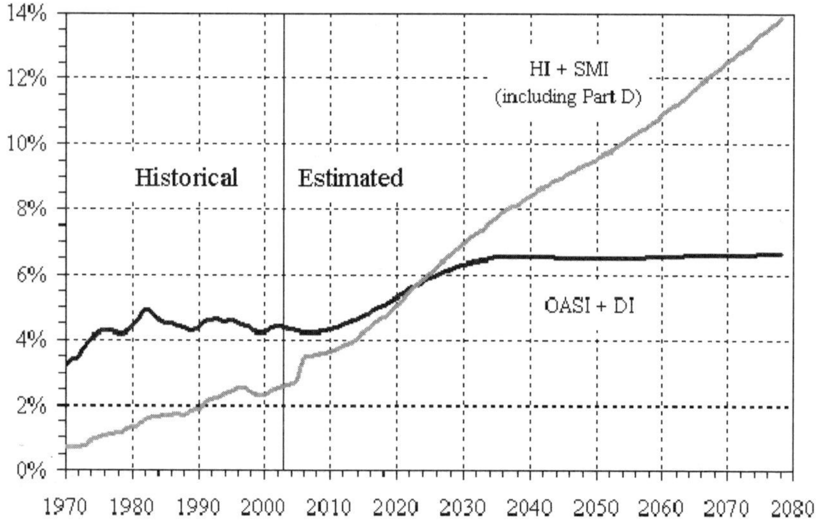

Social Security Administration, 2004

Economists, like Dr. Robert Goodman, warn we are out of options. He says it is unlikely retirees (the majority of the active voters) will accept less, so the only choice is increasing taxes.[70]

"Dr. Bob," as he is cordially known to millions of viewers on television financial news programs, has a bleak picture for the future. He agrees with the view of the situation as presented from the Social Security Trustees. As the tax cuts reach their apex in the pendulum swing, the federal government, out of necessity, will begin its required philosophical change and begin increasing the individual income tax. This will occur at the same time the Baby Boomers will start to retire. Fewer workers mean fewer taxpayers at a time when there is a tremendous need to replace the outflow of Social Security and Medicare funds.

The only logical option to avoid a collapse of the system, as suggested by economists, may be an extraordinary increase in other taxes because there will not be enough individual tax payers to take care of the costs.

One tax that has a built-in "sunset law" is the Estate and Gift Tax. The moment the public starts to realize that they should panic, that tax will be one of the first dominos to fall. Rather than allowing the 50% death tax to drop to zero, as expected in 2010, politicians, as they have for ages, will probably begin pointing fingers trying to avoid the moniker that the other party was responsible for the increase of taxes. Nevertheless, the Estate and Gift Tax will be reinstated. Even though this tax does not bring in much income when compared with other revenue sources, the hard earned estates of the Baby Boomers will possibly see a huge erosion because the Boomers and their parents have already received their benefits. Now it is time for someone to pay.

There are not that many sources of income, so, according to Dr. Goodman, corporations may be hit the hardest.[71] As Congress looks to new sources of funding, both federal and state governments will scramble, looking for ways to increase the revenues. Increased taxes may be required on the backs of corporations.

As corporations struggle under increased taxes, out of necessity, businesses will have to increase their prices to pass the tax on to the consumers.

A big sucking sound may be heard around the world as the stability plug is pulled out of the economic drain holding our market in place. Increased corporate taxes will increase prices, which will increase inflation compounding the potential drop in the economy and the possible fall of the stock market.

06:00

What Gives? The Economic Circle of Life

Retirement. Aches and Pains. Old age. Leisure and maybe Travel. Health Crises. Old-old age. Death.

As predictable as it may seem, life is a constant surprise. Perhaps the reason people are regularly caught unaware is because they secretly hope the personal, financial or health problems other people face will never happen to them.

But the internal clock keeps ticking, and every life goes through some version of the same process. Even though the medical world has been helping the average person live longer by ten to twenty years or more, everyone knows they will die by 85 to 100 years of age.

History does have a way of repeating itself. It is often called a cycle. Just wait long enough and something is bound to happen again. The same is true with the economy. While the "economy" is the big picture, an "investment portfolio" is nothing more than the economy happening on a smaller, personal scale to individual investors.

Comparing the human life cycle with the economy draws at least two disconcerting conclusions to an otherwise oblivious nation: the uncertainty and ambiguity of it all, and the tenuous, fine strand that holds the whole system together.

Big Brother Will Take Care of Me. Maybe.

Living through the Great Depression of the 1930s left its scars on a nation.

One man, identified as "Steve S.," was a teenager in Youngstown, Ohio during that oppressive decade, and told how his parents struggled to provide food for the family, living off their little garden. Occasionally his parents would have enough money to buy a chicken for their Sunday dinner. The majority of families in his community were without employment. In an interview about his impressions and expectations, this is how he responded:

> "Question: How did living through the depression affect the rest of your life?
>
> Steve: In my own case, I have been very careful not to risk any money even in the stock market. I have always invested in treasuries, bank Certificates of Deposit, and savings accounts, which are ensured by the Federal Government. I don't take financial risks now; all of my investments

> are federally ensured (sic). I do not own one stock presently.
>
> Question: Do you believe a depression could reoccur anytime soon?
>
> Steve: I believe it will not reoccur. I believe it will not happen again because the Federal Reserve control of the financial markets, added to the sustained incomes provided by Social Security, are good tools for fighting against another severe depression. People receive Social Security, and spend it."[72]

For over 70 years, many Americans were certain that the deficit spending of President Franklin D. Roosevelt was the answer to their financial troubles. Their firm belief: the Federal Reserve will always "control the financial markets" and Social Security checks will always be there to spend.

Maybe.

In the financial world, looking back through time, economic cycles have been just as regular, and just as uncertain as life. However, it is not an economy that usually dies; the human race is quite resilient as people continue to grow food, make things that others want, trade and consume. All this commerce has gone on whether or not a nation endures. History is full of fallen governments requiring a complete overhaul, often facilitated by civil war or invading armies. But the crash usually occurs only after years of moral decay from within and not from a major economic crisis. The remaining community has normally found some way to go on with life.

Even though 1776 is celebrated as the birth of America, it is usually unknown that the U.S. money system has not had as many years to practice. In comparison, the Federal Reserve life cycle is relatively short. In fact, it is intriguing that Chairman Alan Greenspan would suggest that America's economic future is difficult to envision past the year 2012. The very next year, 2013, the Federal Reserve reaches only its first 100 year anniversary. While it is unlikely that the Fed's lifespan will be as short as the people it serves, it is possible the organization may still experience growing pains, and with it, major health crises.

The Chairman of the Federal Reserve is in an unpleasant spot as he is one of the few financial administrators who are totally responsible for the future of the economy. If he makes a mistake, the whole world feels it. For years, Mr. Greenspan (the Fed Chairman from 1987 to 2008) expressed concern that Americans have not had enough experience to determine what will happen when faced with the potential Baby Boomer crisis.

Reading between the lines, Mr. Greenspan says Americans don't know how young and fragile their financial system really is. In the two decades that he was the adopted parent of the national economy, he wondered aloud before Congressional committees about America's eagerness to believe in the infallibility of their national monetary system, when he saw all the warts and flaws, and knew there was at least another century of insecurity after he left office.

First, the words of the Federal Reserve Chairman, then an interpretation:

> Because we have not experienced a sufficient number of economic turning points to judge the causal linkages among increased globalization, improved monetary policy, significant disinflation, and greater economic stability, the structure of the transitional paradigm is necessarily sketchy.[73]

Simply put, at the turn of the millennium, United States economists have not had enough experience with the monetary system, let alone the worldwide economy, to accurately judge what tomorrow will bring.

Perhaps most Americans will not see this as a pessimistic view because they have grown to have such a tremendous faith in the system and because they have never seen a crash that has not been able to be controlled. Maybe the general public is numbed or has become imprudently optimistic because decades of advertisements have proclaimed their money is safely "Guaranteed" by the United States government; they have come to believe that their monetary system is near perfect and that it could never fail. Perhaps, however, the reason the Fed, and as will be shown later, the FDIC, have been warning about possible failures is because the system has never been tested by a storm like it could experience throughout its second century of existence.

The still-growing U.S. economy has always been in a constant state of flux, always changing, always requiring someone, such as the Fed chairman, to nurse it along.

It doesn't take an economist to recognize that these expansions and contractions are a part of life. As much as constant growth is desired, a contraction or recession in the economy is not something that should be abhorred, rather, it is a fact investors must be willing to accept. It is as normal as breathing.

Occasionally, however, an economic illness may infect the system, causing multiple recessions to spread and develop into the dreaded depression. In this case, most would prefer a professional to treat the disorder. They would rather believe it is a rational, scientific conclusion that will allow the chairman of the Federal Reserve Board to formulate an educated decision to make everything better again.

That's what a doctor does, right? Well, it may not be as simple as that.

An *ARTIST* is Going to Operate on ME?!!?

For many, an economist conjures up memories of a studious-appearing scientist, one who deals with facts and figures. The moderately educated bystander assumes economists are like accountants and should never sway from the truth, because one plus one will always equal two. At least that was the assumption at one time.

However, during the 20th century, the economy showed itself to be downright emotion-driven. Since the 1930s, the federal government has vacillated between two different economic models, the "fiscal policy," which worked very well, until the 1970s, and the "monetary policy".

During the 1990s investors began to think they could never go wrong as the market seemed to be skyrocketing on the back of the new computer technology era. There was serious discussion that the old theories needed to be revamped and replaced because a "new economy" had taken over. But when the market reached its peak in March 2000 economists finally recognized they had been riding an unusually long old-fashioned expansion. Then corporate governance scandals opened the eyes of the public to see that economists and accountants were just as susceptible to error and fraud. Finally, 9/11/ 2001, brought a dark day for Wall Street, New York City, Washington D.C., and America. For nearly three years investors struggled through a suffocating recession and the longest bear market in 70 years. Rather than the giddy optimism of the 1990s, the public became pessimistic and began to question whether the market would ever go up again.

The 2001 recession brought many more to the realization that directing the economy was an art, not a science.

Trying to nail down the causes of a recession, the Congressional Research Service delivered a report to Congress acknowledging that recessions are affected by "confidence, uncertainty, and pessimism."[74] This was the theory of the 1930s British economist, John Maynard Keynes, the father of "fiscal policy". He explained that it was "animal spirits" which drove pessimism; motivated by human emotion and driven by psychology.[75] Embracing "fiscal policy" introduced the acknowledgement of an emotion driven economy. To successfully avoid a depression, as believed for years by the majority of America, the government only had to decrease taxes, encourage spending, and lower interest rates.

This fiscal control worked for forty years till outside economic influences, or an external "shock," such as the combined end of the Vietnam War and the 1970s oil embargo, forged a new controlled approach to drive the economy out of the 1973-75 financial hole. American economist Milton Friedman won the 1976 Nobel Prize when he designed a quantifiable and objective analysis of the economy and named it "monetary policy." This policy, which has become the key to America's financial future, recommends increasing the money supply at a steady rate, all controlled through the increase or decrease of interest rates.

But scientific economic control can only go so far if the "perfect storm" arrives. Consider again, the key ingredients, when combined, that neither a fiscal nor monetary policy alone can fix. The Economists' Economist should be concerned when all the negatives are brought together at once:

- Inflation, high unemployment or under-employment, the psychological impact of a bursting emotional bubble (the lack of confidence, uncertainty, and pessimism),
- Multiple unexpected events, like terrorist attacks, or any number of other uncontrollable shocks (i.e., 46 million potential retirees, a possible drop in the stock market and real estate values),

- Incapability to correct the expected future bankruptcies of federal agencies (Medicare and Social Security).

Alone, any one these problems could be controlled through previously used methods, however, bring them all together at one period of time during a turbulent economic crisis, and this group can be enough to drive the economy into a long term depression.[76] No wonder the future is called "opaque" by the one man who should be able to foretell the coming events.

Some people, without understanding the economic ramifications, might suggest that the government should "Just print more money!" But it isn't as easy as that. Part of the problem of over printing currency resulted in the Panic of 1893 and the severe depression left in its wake. History shows when the government indiscriminately printed paper money, it caused inflation to skyrocket out of control. Such bank panics are caused by both external shocks and the self-fulfilling actions of the depositors.[77]

Each policy, fiscal and monetary, normally acted upon independently by the Fed, can be effectively used to reign in inflation and unemployment, which, if left unchecked, will cause a depression.

This is precisely the reason economists must use an artistic touch when managing the "science" of money. The knowledgeable public assumes it, and the economists admit there is an "art" to forecasting.[78]

A report justifying the value of the Federal Reserve to the Congressional Economic Committee, explained,

"While economists have identified broad principles to guide policymakers, making policy is not a science. Good policy will probably always require good policymakers, as it requires combining the science of the economist with the art of the practitioner."[79]

If the field of economics was a pure science and all that was needed was a steady increase of the money supply, as theorized by Friedman, then we could potentially put all the information into a computer and just work off the raw data. But the 1990s taught us that uncertainty, unbridled optimism, pessimism, and worry of the unknown still required one person with the artist's touch to make the final decision, like the Fed Chairman.

Inflation, Deflation, or Stagflation: Bring It On!

Most people think of inflation and unemployment in negative terms, primarily taught by the media. Yet these economic elements should not be feared because the Federal Reserve Board needs both ingredients to work against each other to manipulate the nation's money system.

Inflation occurs when the average level of prices go up. At the opposite extreme, deflation occurs with the downward movement of the average level of prices. Stagflation is when the whole system is broken with high inflation and high unemployment. That's when economists start pointing their fingers at every one else. (See Appendix 2 for a light analogy on how the economy is like a family).

To understand inflation, all that is necessary is the starting (or Nominal Value) and ending prices (or Real Value). One way to appreciate how nominal and real value work, is to compare movie theater box office receipts. The movie Titanic, by Paramount, was the all-time box office hit with gross sales of over $600 million (by 2004). Way down the list, at number 55, was MGM's Gone with the Wind, at $198 million. At first glance it would appear there was no contest, until it is remembered that Gone with the Wind was released nearly 60 years earlier in 1939.

All Time Box Office Hits[80]

Rank	Film (Year)	$ Domestic Total
1	Titanic (1997)	$600,788,188
2	Star Wars (1977)	$460,998,007
3	Shrek 2 (2004)	$440,856,541
4	E.T. The Extra-Terrestrial (1982)	$435,110,554
5	Star Wars: EP.1 (1999)	$431,088,301
6	Spider-Man (2002)	$403,706,375
7	Lord of the Rings: Return of the King (2003)	$377,027,325
8	Spider-Man 2 (2004)	$373,377,893
9	The Passion of the Christ (2004)	$370,274,604
10	Jurassic Park (1993)	$357,067,947

All Time Box Office Hits Adjusted for Inflation[81]

Rank	Film (Year)	Adjusted Gross	Unadjusted Gross
1	Gone With the Wind (1939)	$1,240,554,000	$198,676,459
2	Star Wars (1977)	$1,093,654,300	$460,998,007
3	Sound of Music (1965)	$ 874,430,400	$158,671,368
4	E.T (1982)	$ 870,985,600	$435,110,554
5	The Ten Commandments (1956)	$ 804,340,000	$ 65,500,000
6	Titanic (1997)	$ 788,043,700	$600,788,188
7	Jaws (1975)	$ 786,403,900	$260,000,000
8	Dr. Zhivago (1965)	$ 762,191,700	$111,721,910
9	The Exorcist (1973)	$ 678,891,600	$232,671,011
10	Snow White (1937)	$ 669,260,000	$184,925,486

The method of measuring inflation is called a Price Index. This is the cost of the goods or services today as compared to its cost at any given time in the past as the point of reference. When the media reports the Consumer Price Index (CPI), the Producer Price Index (PPI), or the Gross Domestic Product Deflator, the government is simply reporting on the statistical measure of a specified set of goods and services expected to be purchased by a particular group.

The CPI compares goods and services purchased by wage earners in urban areas. The PPI is designed to analyze the sales from manufacturers to wholesalers or retailers. The GDP is the broadest measure of prices which is not based on any one given end user.

Understanding the business cycles and being prepared for them is essential in financial planning. Any healthy economy requires both expansion and contraction, but a recession can occur when the rate of growth of business activity is consistently less than the long-term trend or is negative. A depression is simply an extremely severe recession.

The See Saw Economy

During the Great Depression in the 1930s, unemployment weighed on the nation as a quarter of the national workforce was without a job.[82] In some industrial areas, like Youngstown, Ohio, that number soared to three times the national average as thousands of families went without.[83] The Keynesian Policy was successful as President Roosevelt's administration decreased taxes and increased spending by putting millions of people back to work.

Jobs were created to build new dams and highways and other roadways, set up huge government departments (such as the 1935 Social Security Act), and countless other federal projects. Increased federal spending created jobs and put people back to work, which in turn provided a rejuvenated work force and additional tax revenue for the system.

As with anything, but unproven theories, everything breaks down, including social and economic policies[84] which attempt to control the United States monetary system. So Professor Friedman theorized that a constant trickle of money into the economy would be the answer. Although the monetary policy seems to be an important factor to steady the system, after the 1990s it was apparent Friedman's economic policy could not own stabilize the economy on its own.

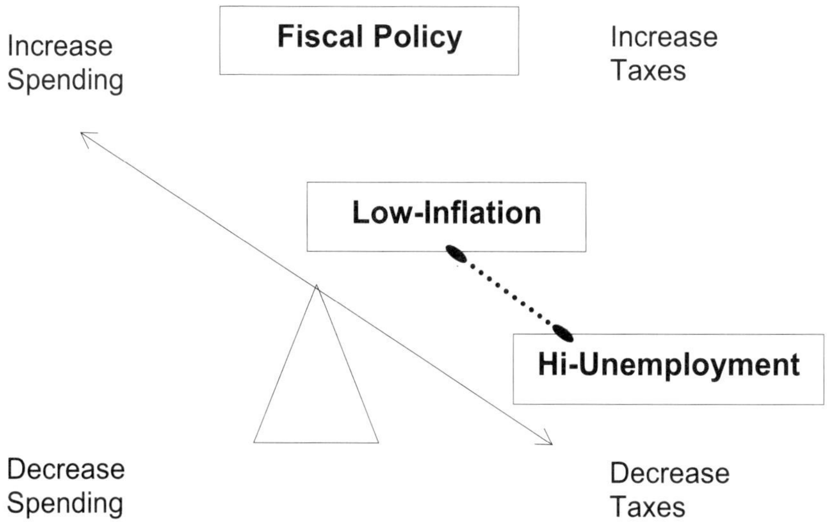

Perhaps an economic equilibrium of sorts will someday be discovered. But will the human race ever be happy with status quo? It is a fact that opposition is required in everything. If you attend a concert, you can only sit so long listening to the beautiful music. Eventually you have to head to the powder room, or to your own comfortable bed. So, rather than the Fed Chairman trying to find the perfect answer to keep the paying audience always in their seat, perhaps this grand conductor of the economy will need to be content with the role of janitor, locking the doors to the orchestral hall at specified times, then sending the audience home to wait for another evening of glorious music.

Maybe the Fed Chairman must be an artist, conductor, or performer who can pull off an economic balancing act between unemployment and inflation, keeping the two interlinked, evenly moving them back and forth between whatever is considered high and low percentages at the time. The fiscal policy (working on the human-nature side of the economy) is best suited to fight unemployment, but the monetary policy seems to be more effective in controlling inflation.[85]

The see-saw economy scale moves in the direction of the policymakers' fiscal or monetary decisions. When inflation is not a problem, but unemployment is high, the Federal Reserve uses fiscal policy to move the scales to decrease taxes and increase the amount of money put into government programs. As in the past, when the government takes this aggressive position of deficit spending, the result is large government budgets providing payrolls to stimulate further consumer spending.

The fiscal button can not permanently be switched on. Even though increased spending decreases unemployment, it actually encourages inflation to escalate. As inflation increases and unemployment drops to a manageable level, then government analysts are required to implement the monetary policy formula by increasing interest and taxes to slow down the growth of the economy.

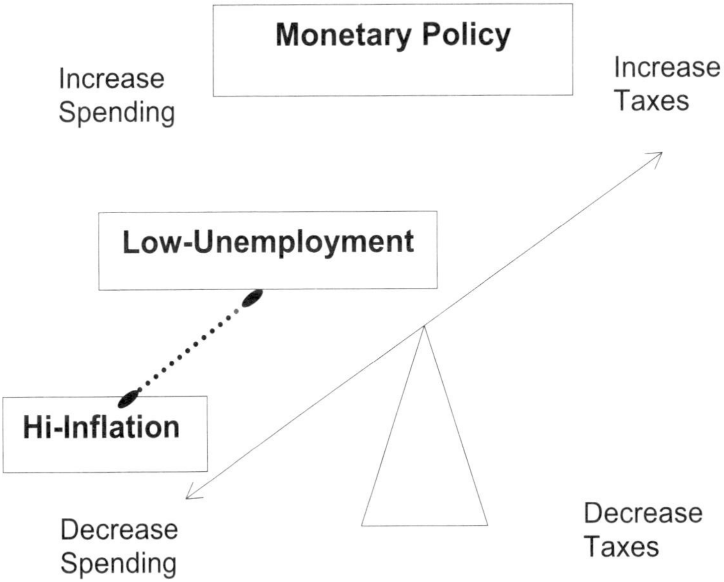

The stable economy, wished for by economists, would see a moderate amount of governmental spending with fair and balanced taxes. The hopeful result would be an ideal inflation level and just enough unemployment to stimulate moderate corporate growth which would drive the economy. At least that is the dream.

The one result economists don't want is a broken scale which is called "stagflation" or "stagnation." This is the worst case scenario where high inflation and high unemployment occur at the same time, slowing down corporate growth, and at the same time, causing a rise in prices. When oil prices shot skyward in the 1970s, costs of living went with it and slowed down the economy. Inflation was made even worse by stagflation.

Stagflation, of this sort, would burst the real estate bubble, possibly sending all the markets into a dive. Fixed Income and bond prices could drop with a very negative affect on the nation's pocketbook and possibly cause some banks to go insolvent. According to some economists, the only way to stop the freefall would be to stop monetary inflation. The result would be a very sharp recession and stock market crash similar to the Great Depression.[86]

Stability is the one goal hoped for by the Federal Reserve. But even though the economist's preference is a stable interest rate and employment environment, that world has yet to take shape over an extended period of time, and in the long run, it may actually be undesirable. In the late 1990s some suggested America had entered a "New Economy" where the financial system was moving at an unusually strong growth rate. And at the same time, this new "structural shift," as described by Alan Greenspan, brought with it low inflation and low unemployment. The forecasters became concerned that the United States could end up with too few new employees to enter the workplace, which could, as economists warn, "drive up wages, trigger inflation, and prompt the Federal Reserve to engineer an economic slowdown."[87]

Think about it: too many retirees and not enough capable workers to replace them.

It will be a college graduate's dream come true. Wages will dramatically increase as recruiters will scramble for a decreasing number of qualified employees. But the paycheck will not go as far as hoped, because, in addition to increasing taxes, corporations will be required to pass along the extra expenses in the cost of durable goods and services, which will be recognized as inflation.

The perfect financial storm could be brought on every which way the Fed turns.

Emotional and financial preparation will be the only keys to withstanding the Real Time Bomb. There are ways to prepare, but you must start now by knowing what the problem could be, and then doing something about it.

And putting all your money into real estate may not be the best idea, either.

07:00

The Real Estate Bubble

Wake up and smell the coffee or burning toast!

WAKE UP!

Life just doesn't go on without a cyclic downer every once in a while.

We don't always breathe in. We do get sick.

We do make dumb decisions on occasion. We might get audited by the IRS.

We do have accidents. We do stub our toes and get wrinkles and put on weight and get old. Sometimes our health is not always going to be perfect, and there is a chance that we could break a hip, get cancer, or have a stroke.

We don't always live. There comes a time when we die.

There comes a time when our loved ones die.

While we face uncertainty and pessimism on a daily basis, there must be some animal instinct within us where we just want to believe in the magical land of Oz. There must be some great wizard out there going to make everything better. But at the end of the dream, we draw back the curtain to find an old, worn out civil servant, pulling the strings, wishing the same dream we dream.

The financial world was living a dream-come-true in the 1990s. Nearly 120 months of constant stock market growth. Some thought it would never bust. It was the "New Economy." But the stock market did contract. It did drop by over a third.

In the early 2000s large numbers of people say the same about real estate. Yes, they admit, there have been cycles in the past, but this time "it is different."

No, Dorothy, this time it is not different. Sooner or later, the wonderful ride up the real estate value line may come to a screeching halt and start to go back down the other side of the slope.

If it happens during the "perfect storm" it is possible that rather than floating, your overly mortgaged home could become an anchor, a noose tied around your neck potentially dragging you down to bankruptcy.

Many real estate owners, with rose colored glasses, argue to the contrary. They assert, "Things are different, now. Things have changed." They say real estate is so much more dependable than the stock market.

Alan Greenspan brings us back from Oz to reality:

> "Has something fundamental happened to the U.S. economy and by extension, U.S. banking, that enables us to disregard all the time tested criteria of imbalance and economic danger? Regrettably, the answer is no. The free lunch has still to be invented."[88]

This time may be different, though. It may be worse than we expected!

POP Goes The Bubble!

Look back to the Great Depression. Most analysts suggest the sharp drop and all the bankruptcies partially occurred because margin loans were so easy to get. When the market reached its peak, it naturally began to contract, to come back down the other side of the slope. But as it did, thousands of investors hoping to make a fast buck on Easy Street, had their margin loans called. They had to sell their other stock positions fast, because that was the rule. It did nothing but cause a dramatic downward crash. Since that time, the federal government organized the Securities and Exchange Commission (SEC) which monitors margin loans to make certain an account never exceeds its ability to pay back its loan.

It is unfortunate, but we may have put ourselves in the same precarious position with real estate. We have unwittingly set the stage for the possibility of another big crash.

Consider this possible scenario:

- The real estate market has outpaced inflation for years, in some cases by more than 300% since 1980.
- Homeowners actually consider real estate conservative and "safe," while the Securities Exchange Commission, and other regulatory agencies consider it a more risky investment, often due to the long period of time required to sell real property.
- At the same time Americans increased their credit card debt load, their home values shot upward.
- Interest rates dropped to a dramatic low, the "lowest in 45 years".
- Homeowners rushed to their mortgage lender to take advantage of the low, low rates.
- Homeowners refinanced, sometimes three, four, and five times just because they could get a lower interest rate.
- Because home and land values had appreciated so dramatically over a twenty year period, there was substantial equity built up.
- Rather than leaving that equity alone, mortgage brokers figured a way to market their easy money by offering a way to pay off business or personal credit card debt by rolling the debt into the equity of the home loan, up to 120%. While they were at it, there was enough to squeeze in the purchase of a big SUV (Sport Utility Vehicle).
- If they were really good, the real estate and mortgage broker sold the homeowner on becoming a landlord by using their equity as a down payment on another highly inflated property. "But," was their persuasive argument, "your renters will make all the payments for you!"

Millions followed this pattern, just like the 1920s when so many investors found out about the great idea to get a loan to buy even more stock, all in the name of getting rich. It was nothing more than slimy, gritty, greed.

Now, consider the following possible slide down the other side of this slippery slope.

- A peak is reached in the real estate market. It can happen for any number of reasons:
  - Sooner or later a peak naturally happens.
  - As in the past, real estate follows the same path as the stock market, only a few years later. The stock market dropped, so can the real estate market once it reaches its peak.
  - Interest rates rise, buyers become more hesitant, and are not so ready to pay top dollar. The housing market hits its peak.
  - 46 million Baby Boomers retire. Most are homeowners. Many want to cut back on their spending, or on the size of their home. They put the home up for sale, looking for 23 million others who want to buy, but the buyers are out looking for the best bargain. The buyers decide to wait for prices to come down from its peak.
- As part of the cycle, prices take their natural course downward. The stock market dropped more than 30%. The real estate market could drop that much, as well.
- Many homeowners, with maximized loans, have little equity left.
- The "liquidity trap" becomes the "equity trap". In a simplified example, lenders, by contract, require

the homeowner to keep at least their fair market value, or to pay up the difference in the loan. But the value is no longer there. One year ago, the loan and home was valued at $200,000, now its fair market value is only $140,000 (a 30% drop in price).

- The lender calls the loan.
- In a bind, the homeowner decides to get a personal loan, because just a few months earlier junk mail offers were available for large amounts of credit. However, now, there is no money available, because their credit rating has dropped due to the huge liability they have on the home.
- Because the government backed the homeowner's mortgage the borrower can keep the home but step out of the loan through bankruptcy. But the government now has to pay off the balance of the loan. Companies like Fannie Mae and Freddie Mac now start to see their values plummet as their assets drop with the bankrupt mortgages.
- Landlords struggle with their mortgage payments as the owners are required to come up with $60,000 to replace the equity or sell the home. They don't get the same break as homeowners do from the bankruptcy laws.
- Other homes in the neighborhood go up for sale for the same reason. The 30% drop escalates.

If the scenario is extended out to other possibilities, the real estate bubble could have far reaching consequences. The emotional drain is enough to cause the stock market to drop. As homeowners start tapping all their resources, including their investment and retirement accounts, the sell off will be enough to cause a significant drop in the economy.

There may come a time when we wish that we had our home paid off, and had not listened to those real estate gurus encouraging huge debt just because "leveraging" is so easy.

There may come a time when we wondered why we listened to the bank, or our friend at the water cooler, and incorrectly put our money into a dead end double payment plan to quickly pay off our mortgage, especially, when we find out that was just another way for the bank to take more money from our pocket book.

There may also come a time, as the lender is repossessing our house, when we wish that we had not taken out that low interest loan on 120% of the value of our home so we could get a "screamin' deal" to pay off our huge credit card debt.

Why would the bank ever do that? They could, they sometimes can, and they would if the opportunity was there. The bank is in business to make money and to turn a profit for its owners.

Overbuilt for the Economic Neighborhood?

When in the market for a new car, most prospective buyers look under the hood, take a test drive, and check into what others say about its benefits and features. Then comes the shock of driving it off the lot and realizing that it just lost ten to twenty percent of its value.

Purchasing real estate also requires a certain amount of checking around. The last thing a buyer wants is to find that the home has problems or its fancy frills have inflated its price above the values of other homes in the neighborhood. When the day comes to sell the owner realizes no one else is willing to pay the expected price.

Although it is obvious, the bottom line to owning real estate is to divide the long-term emotionally held property from that owned for investment. If the real estate is a primary residence, the goal is to have it paid off, because then nothing is owed but real estate tax. If the property is for investment, that is another story. Whether its growth is affected by emotion driven development (speculation), or the regional or national economy (inflation or deflation), the primary investment issue is to know when to sell.

While the regional real estate booms are impossible to gage, the national economic picture, although fuzzy, is more discernible.

Inflation or deflation is usually communicated as the movement of the core consumer price index. However, there are any number of major inflationary pressures which are not considered core, such as the fluctuating value of raw land or new construction projects. Rather than speculation, development projects are the driving force in the increased value of land. However, in many communities prime land is being gobbled up by developers, causing nearby properties, at one time almost impossible to be given away, to escalate to unheard of prices.[89]

Percentage Increase in Housing Prices by Region

Census Division	2002	1998-2002	Since 1980
National	6.9	38.3	184.9
New England	10.6	62.9	356.8
Middle Atlantic	9.9	43.3	256.2
Pacific	9.8	53.4	245.2
South Atlantic	7.0	36.0	173.6
West N. Central	5.6	37.3	146.6
Mountain	4.0	30.2	156.9
East N. Central	4.0	27.8	167.4
West S. Central	3.7	28.0	82.6
East S. Central	3.2	22.6	135.5

Source: Office of Federal Housing Enterprise Oversight, House Price Index, March 2003. Note: Price increases are not adjusted for inflation.

Once again, the Northeast, Middle Atlantic and California are experiencing dramatic property inflation. These regions are where the greatest amount of national wealth is accumulated. If the bubble bursts in these areas many homeowners may be required to cash out their investments to offset the loss.

So, that raises the question, is there a Real Estate Bubble? In 2002, the Chairman of Freddie Mac, said, "In my opinion, the answer is simply "no".[90] He then went on to enumerate the reasons, such as low inventory, low interest rates, etc.

While disagreement is healthy, there is cause for concern when some of the most influential financial leaders attempt to diminish needless worry at the expense of being prepared.

In reality, most economists currently believe bubbles can not be identified until after the burst.[91] There are too many factors influencing the marketplace at any one time to be able to adequately warn of an impending collapse. But still, the signs are there, and caution is prudent. When a vehicle is speeding and comes upon slippery conditions, it only makes sense that the driver should slow down to save lives.

In a significant Congressional Report, analysts presented a sobering forecast. In 2003, the real value of homes was 22% lower than the national average selling price. Some regions, such as the dry, undesirable plains of Texas, hundreds of miles from developed property or oil rich reserves, have seen a decrease in value over a twenty year period,[92] while real estate in other regions have exploded five to six times more than the cost of inflation.[93] The property values in California, with eight of the top ten markets in the nation, makes up a sizable fraction of the country's real estate.[94] A spillover effect is driving the market in those regions as many homeowners in California, New England, and New York sell out and move to neighboring states, causing the property value to escalate wherever they go.

With all this activity, the federal report gives the following ominous warning:

> If housing prices were being driven by a bubble, there is a chance that they could suddenly collapse, with adverse effects on the U.S. economy. Residential investment could fall significantly. A decline in housing wealth could depress consumption, thereby depressing aggregate spending in the short run. A sudden collapse in housing prices could also affect the health of the financial sector if

> financial institutions are not adequately safeguarded. All of these possibilities give Congress a cause for concern, yet effective policy responses to a bubble are difficult. If house prices were to decline in some regions, it would not be the first time this occurred....
>
> Recalling the behavior of the stock market in late 1990s, some analysts fear that the recent appreciation in housing prices points to a price bubble, or a rise in house prices that cannot be explained by fundamentals. Instead, prices could be driven by 'irrational exuberance.' If housing prices were being driven by a bubble, there is a chance that they could suddenly collapse, with adverse effects on the U.S. economy.[95]

The final analysis of this report presented to congress proposed the financial system would only be hurt if "homeowners responded by defaulting on existing loans."[96] However, a regional or national economic crisis, namely, a depression, unemployment, coupled with high inflation, would be enough of a reason for homeowners to default on their mortgage payments.

The Perfect Real Estate Storm

Once again, it is unlikely that real estate will collapse all on its own. Mr. Greenspan has assured America that while some metropolitan areas may experience a bloated market, the nation as a whole does not need to worry.[97] Some people, with property in highly desirable locations feel there will always be someone who will pay inflated prices for their property. But that philosophy could also have caused an "irrational exuberance" in the mortgage and real estate market boom. Too often, investors live in a land of denial, where they staunchly proclaim, "It will never happen here."

Few people ever live in a bubble; rather they exist on the outside. Real estate, at the turn of the millennium, is like a taut balloon in a nail factory being blown about by every wind of fortune. Investors want to believe their bed of nails is so tightly compact that those sharp points would never dare puncture the delicate skin of their market. But what they don't see may hurt them. Because, over time, some of the points rust, get brittle, and under pressure collapse, allowing the small prick of a few to affect the many.

Some Realtors recognize the uncertainty of it all. Calling it "The Perfect Real Estate Storm," columnist Blanche Evans, writing for the real estate industry[98], suggests the following problems may lead to widespread instability in the housing market:

- Jobs - A slowing housing market will hurt multiple industries, such as "mortgage lending, real estate sales, furniture sales, building, contracting, moving, and other jobs."
- Flat Housing Market – June 15th, 2004, Federal Reserve Chairman Alan Greenspan testified to U.S. senators, "We perceive that the very strong expansion in new and existing home sales is now flattening out. And the really quite unexpected boom in home sales over the recent years is unlikely to be continued. Our forecast is generally

flat, not in prices but in aggregate volumes. Where house prices go, I'm not sure, but I would be quite surprised if they showed continued acceleration on the upside."[99]

- Inflation – History, and common sense, tells us that houses should stay one or two percentage points ahead of the Consumer Price Index. But the rates, in some cases are 60% to 300% more.
- Housing affordability – A magazine marketed to Canadian accountants[100], suggests the problem of overpriced homes is not only a problem in the U.S. In 2004, the bubble is "fit to burst" — as the cost of a home is far over real value throughout many parts of the world as "average prices were overvalued by 16%, peaking at 30% in such places as the Netherlands, Great Britain and Australia. In those countries, nominal prices jumped 100% to 125%." Some American economists forecast housing prices to drop by 10% or more.
- House Poor – "One in six homes in the U.S. are sold in California, so when housing affordability is an issue there, it impacts housing across the nation. A recent June report stated that less than 20 percent of households can afford the median-priced home in California." The median-priced home in California in 2004 was $453,590 requiring a family income of $102,550 to pay for the average.[101]
- Overburdened consumer – The average consumer is strapped with large credit card debt. Interest rate increases can slow down spending, which could lead to further job loss.
- Debt service - CBS Marketwatch chief economist Dr. Irwin Kellner in February 2004, said consumer debt reached nearly $9.2 trillion. This

record is 110 percent of people's take-home pay adjusted for inflation. "Ten years ago, household debt equaled 85 percent of disposable personal incomes; twenty years ago it was 65 percent."[102] To put it into perspective, all the real estate loans over a ten year period (1994-2003) came to a total of $15 trillion.[103]

- Easy loans -- Easy credit, leads to easy money, resulting in not-so-easy debt. The number of Adjustable Rate Mortgages (ARMs) is at an all time high. Low interest rates now, mean higher rates later, and higher mortgage payments, and a potential of an increase in bankruptcies.
- High tapped-equity asking prices – Economist, Dean Baker, states, "The ratio of mortgage debt to home equity is at record highs. This fact is especially scary given that equity values may be inflated by as much as 20 to 30 percent as a result of the housing bubble, and that the nation's demographics (with the Baby Boomers approaching retirement) suggest that many homeowners should have largely paid off their mortgages."

Real estate columnist, Evans, concludes, “Some of these conditions have existed before. Inflation was slowed by rising interest rates that capped at 19 percent in the 1980s, but homebuyers weren't facing higher costs along with on-our-own-turf terrorism, crushing consumer debt, and the worst job market in decades, along with all these other factors at the same time.”[104]

Real estate investors should keep a national, long-term perspective in mind. There is value in taking a step back, even if it is across the street, to get a view of the big picture, to make certain that now is the right time to make a long term commitment. Remember that with the aging of America, there will be a major shift in the way people live:

- More than one-fourth of all households (27.2%), in the 2000 Census, are made up of one person. In 1940, only 8 percent of the households were single person dwellings.[105]
- The elderly living alone are mostly women. The Census Bureau reports most homeowners are men, while most elderly who live alone are women who will need large retirement communities to provide the necessary long term care support.[106]
- As the population of the United States grows older, the real estate market will be affected as the size of households shrink due to lower fertility rates. In the future there will become a need for what is described as "multi-generational housing." This household is one where the under-65 age group will be responsible for caring for the older age group.[107]

The real estate market will see many additional changes, some too ambiguous to predict, the closer the Baby Boomers get to retirement. Economists in California are concerned that one of the main drivers of the skyrocketing real estate market is greed feeding upon itself. Dr. Edward Leamer gives notice that the "recent surge in prices have created a clear bubble in prices and eventually there needs to be some return to sustainable price levels -- likely when interest rates rise again."[108]

Perhaps one of the difficult forecasts to make is trying to identify what an unstable economy will do to the mega mortgage corporations set up by the government. Trillions of dollars are held by the federally backed gigantic mortgage-cousins Fannie Mae and Freddie Mac. During what Mr. Greenspan called an "exceptionally mild recession"[109] (the Recession from 2001 to 2003) these two huge lenders of most of the home loans in the country showed a chink in their armor.

To cover their back sides, the Senate Banking Committee began the process of protecting the public if these two mortgage holders should go bankrupt.[110] While the mortgage giants are trying to convince the nation that nothing is wrong, that everything will be fine, politicians on both sides of the aisle are warning about the potential collapse of Fannie Mae and Freddie Mac.

One huge concern for the stability of the economy is that these two government fed monstrosities, which hold the mortgages on millions of homes, "have grown so big that they pose a systemic risk to the US financial system."[111] The Senate Banking Committee recognizes the potential pit that the country could fall into without a way to get out of the bankruptcy of these government sponsored enterprises. The banking committee has attempted to provide a way for the government to avoid a federal bailout if either Freddie Mac or Fannie Mae should ever become insolvent.[112]

This means that rather than 100% of the public being responsible to pay for the failure of the mortgage companies, only the portion of the country which has a mortgage and has been naïve enough to be caught with mortgage backed bonds will be forced to pay. The unfortunate part of this nightmare is the fact that most of America has a mortgage, and a majority has their money tied up with these companies. If Americans have not invested in bonds, or bond mutual funds, their banks have!

Meanwhile, the federal government guarantees Financial Institutions (Commercial Banks, Savings and Loans, Credit Unions), Government Sponsored Enterprises (Fannie Mae, Freddie Mac, Farm Credit System, Federal Home Loan Banks), Private Employer Pension Funds, Non-Financial Firms (Small Business Administration Loans, Farms, Large Commercial Enterprises), and Households (FHA, VA, and RHS Guaranteed Mortgages, Student Loans) among others.

This promise amounts to at least $9.2 trillion dollars "guaranteed" by the federal government. Nearly one-fourth of all liabilities is protected by the taxpayer. If a there was a "systemic" crash caused by both the stock market and real estate market dropping at once, the government has insured it could be a big one!

Inflation Redistributes Wealth

The Federal Reserve Bank of San Francisco provides the following scenario when describing how falling real estate prices, can lead to deflation, which can lead to a depression:

> Deflation can be as bad as too much inflation. And the reasons are pretty similar. For example, to go back to the case of the fixed-rate loan, a surprise deflation also redistributes wealth, but in the opposite direction from inflation, that

> is, from borrowers to lenders. The reason is that deflation raises the real burden of making a stream of payments whose nominal value is fixed.
>
> A substantial, prolonged deflation, like the one during the Great Depression, can be associated with severe problems in the financial system. It can lead to significant declines in the value of collateral owned by households and firms, making it more difficult to borrow. And falling collateral values may force lenders to call in outstanding loans, which would force firms to cut back their scale of operations and force households to cut back consumption.
>
> Finally, in a deflationary episode, interest rates are likely to be lower than they are during periods of low inflation, which means that the Fed's ability to stimulate the economy will be even more limited.[113]

The Federal Deposit Insurance Corporation has a phrase for the giant banks of the world, “TBTF” or “Too Big To Fail.”[114]

Perhaps another phrase should be “WOB” for “Watch Out Below!”

08:00

FDIC: The "Moral Hazard"

"You've got to be kidding! Why wouldn't someone in their right mind want Certificate of Deposit rates like that? That CD rate is fantastic! You can't beat it anywhere! And on top of that it's guaranteed! It's safe! It's protected by the FDIC!!!"

This response, ladies and gentlemen, is what is called "Moral Hazard".

Now, most people are going to say, "So! What is wrong with that? The government wouldn't guarantee something that wasn't 'rock solid', right?"

Well, yes and no. First of all, those "great rates" are normally not made available through the best banks. In our competitive economy it would seem any bank, credit union, or thrift bank would want to attract business by paying aggressive rates. But instead, most well run banks pay low interest rates to safeguard their client's assets. Second, many depositors are willing to ignore the flashing neon *RISK* sign because their belief is that the government will be there to make everything better if the bank goes broke. And third, as will be shown in the following pages, the FDIC is not what most people hope it is.

In 1933, the Federal Deposit Insurance Corporation (FDIC) was designed to restore public confidence in banks, prevent panics, and to protect less sophisticated depositors. But as the Federal Reserve has warned, too much government helps encourage large banks to invest their assets in high risk securities, putting their clients in danger of losing money.[115] This aggressive investment style leads to what is called "moral hazard" because a 100% guarantee, in a competitive environment, may persuade bank managers to ignore safe havens for higher paying ventures.

For decades, economists have been concerned about the behavior the FDIC is encouraging. The bank creates a moral hazard when management, trying to attract as much business as possible, places their assets in risky investments. The customers, assuming all banks are alike because of the implied government protection, open their accounts at institutions which may pay higher interest rates, without reviewing the bank's financial records. And finally, the federal government, attempting to keep both lobbyists and voters happy, oversteps its ability to protect by promising to pay for everyone's indiscretions.

As economists look back on the 1980s banking crisis, they admit this is one of the very issues that caused the FSLIC to go bankrupt. Remember? The Federal Savings and Loan Insurance Corporation was the

FDIC's sibling agency that got caught in the swirling 1980s real estate market and was flushed down the drain with billions of taxpayer's dollars as it slipped into history, bankrupt.

Past chairman of the FDIC, L. William Seidman, gave the following perplexing view of the organization entrusted to him:

> A deposit insurance system is like a nuclear power plant. If you build it without safety precautions, you know it's going to blow you off the face of the earth. And even if you do, you can't be sure it won't.[116]

The bottom line for the future: Buyer Beware.

The Bigger They Are....

As part of the temporary plastic surgery performed on the FDIC in 1991, a few dozen super large banks were given the coveted title of "TBTF," or "Too Big To Fail." Unfortunately, this moniker aggravates the moral hazard question as it seems to give a false sense of security because the government promises the banks to protect all their assets, whether or not they meet federal depository standards.[117] These banks were important enough to the national economy that the taxpayers promised, through Congress, to step in and lend a helping hand, no matter how deep the financial hole the banks were stuck in.

But the old adage of "the bigger the better" may not be true when it comes to the banking industry. In fact, since about a dozen banks hold the vast majority of America's money, there is the possibility that they could actually be "top heavy," primed to be toppled. Specifically, according to economist Arthur E. Wilmarth, Jr., writing for the International Monetary Fund, these huge mega-banks have an insatiable desire for an ever-larger market share which results in "higher leverage, less liquidity and a more risky asset-liability mix."[118] The problem that faces taxpayers in the United States is that just one major bank failure could bankrupt the FDIC.[119]

Economists and other commentators use the phrase "systemic risk" to describe the potential collapse of the economy: if one big domino falls, all the others could go with it. The government's philosophy behind depository insurance is to have multiple banks equally responsible for protecting the nation from utter financial chaos.

The mechanism of protecting the whole system from collapse is similar to a break in a large reservoir. However, rather than having only one potential direction for the water to flow, the FDIC's ideal plan would channel the flow equally to a number of strong dams down river which would be able to collect the overflow and stop it before it reaches the unsuspecting masses in the cities below.

But according to many economists, this idealistic plan is not necessarily realistic.

In today's consolidation of super-banks, most financial institutions have interconnected liabilities and loans structured within large holding companies. Since these huge corporations normally own unrelated subsidiaries, the secondary divisions may rely on the support of their parent corporation at the first sign of trouble. If the public gets wind of the parent bank's struggles it could set off a "flight to safety" throughout the entire banking, insurance, and securities industries.[120] Economists are concerned, in the case of a destabilizing corporate structure, federal regulators would be forced to step in to avoid the potential corporate meltdown.

The simultaneous collapse of Japan's real estate and stock markets in the early 1990s crippled the banks and left no substantial alternative source of financing for Japanese businesses. "Accordingly, the Japanese experience provides a clear warning signal about the potential for systemic risk that may already exist within U.S. and European LCBOs [large complex banking organizations]."[121] Dr. Wilmarth concludes,

> The unmistakable lesson of the past three decades is that regulators will protect major financial firms against failure whenever such action is deemed necessary to preserve the stability of the capital markets. As a consequence, financial institutions understand that they can increase their leverage and pursue more risky activities as they grow in size and complexity. Without a comprehensive reform of the current regulatory structure, LCBOs [large complex banking organizations] will continue to exploit the subsidies provided under the TBTF policy and other components of the federal safety net.[122]

The potential problem facing the U.S. and world economies is the risky interconnected loans of the holding companies which have already filled the down-river reservoirs to the brim, like a large submerged balloon which takes up space in the water without providing any mass. When the up-river dam collapses, the other walls may not be able to hold the torrent back, causing the down-river structures to collapse under stress.

It's NOT the "FDI-Agency"

FDIC economists have long used the term "moral hazard" to describe the tendency of banks to relax their moral obligation to be safe. This encourages the financial organizations to sell off assets, making their balance sheets look better, all because management knows "big brother" is there to catch their fall if someone makes a wrong decision. Moral hazard also occurs with the client depositors, who are more interested in the free toaster, and do not take the time to analyze the quality of the bank's assets.[123] Because of this guarantee, the American public has a sense of security, believing the government will not hesitate to protect them.

Meanwhile, most people have no idea the "C" in FDIC stands for "Corporation." Why would the 1933 U.S. Congress make this federal agency a corporation? What do corporations do? They either succeed or fail. Because there is no profit motive on the part of the FDIC, there is only one other reason for the creation of this corporate safety net: it is designed to protect the public while protecting the government from possible collapse.[124]

There are some who will be disbelieving and unhappy with the suggestion there could be anything wrong with the Federal Deposit Insurance Corporation. It is true, as it currently stands, there is probably no better program operating in the world to protect depositors – barring a few adjustments. Since President Roosevelt signed the Banking Act in 1933 which created the FDIC, not one person in the United States has ever lost a dime.[125]

But the success of the past does not mean the future will always be the same. The people who lived at the base of Mount Vesuvius were certain it would never erupt. Looking back, we know otherwise. And when was the last time someone said, "There is nothing certain in life but death, taxes and the FDIC"? It is not said because everyone knows there are some things in life that can not be promised, other than death and taxes.

The purpose of this discussion is not to pick apart a system that has provided a phenomenal service. The intention is to step outside of the economist-talk about Moral Hazard,[126] and to be a warning voice of the <u>potential</u> time bomb that faces the country's mortgages and checking accounts.

Some economists point to the excellent FDIC track record and suggest that federalist regulation is the reason for its safety. However, other economists warn that Americans should not be so certain of their seemingly indestructible economy. Reports show that banks, from 1933 to 1965, tended to fail more often in the heavily regulated United States monetary system than in the regulation-free economies of Canada and Hong Kong.[127] The studies do not suggest that there were no problems present in the foreign economies during these years. The point to be stressed is the U.S. depositor should not be smug and assume that their economic system is the only one that works.

The fact that the 1933 banking act created the FDIC as a corporation underscores the obvious fact, whether federally protected or not, the entity (the corporation) can make wrong moves or the external economy around it can move upon it, potentially causing it to collapse, requiring a taxpayer bailout. History shows that the government allowed the FSLIC to come unglued. There is always the possibility that the same can happen to the FDIC.

Is The FDIC Guaranteed to Never Fail?

Congress has given the FDIC an extremely tenuous tightrope on which to balance. The sharks below are circling, waiting. Just as old sport stars finally show their age, so this agency is showing its frailties even though America still expects it to be the ageless superhero to what ails the country. It is not that the FDIC did not have superhero status in the past. It has proven it can effortlessly climb economic walls and swing from financial skyscrapers. In fact, at times it has appeared to be faster than a speeding bullet, or able to jump tall buildings with a single bound. But wise and experienced its directors may be, it has its limits. There are signs that an unexpected dose of economic "kryptonite" could cause the FDIC's knees to buckle and stumble.

Has the United States government created an agency that can never fail? The answer is, no.

The fact that Corporations fail and the FDIC is a corporation should not cause the public to go running about in panic. The FDIC has a huge national constituency backing it. But there are other options available that provide safeguards which will be discussed later. The key to the reality of today's financial world is attentive Preparation.

While most agree a "moral hazard" exists, there are some who view the FDIC as more than a hazard and call for major reform, if not its total abolishment. One president of a major bank described the agency, in a letter to the Federal Reserve warning, "The deposit insurance system is indeed a monster and it is a monster that threatens to devour the very system it is intended to protect."[128]

There will always be someone with a conflicting view. Just because there is a theory, opinion, or philosophy floating around does not mean it is right. But when the FDIC spends large sums of money to encourage outside economists to review and analyze its operations, it is vital that the country does not turn away, assuming every critique is heard, acted upon, and all is well. There is no ideal agency, and as the following discussion details, it is apparent the FDIC is far from perfect.

History Lessons Unlearned

The depositing public assumes the FDIC will take care of them no matter what happens. But history has shown if there is trouble, the taxpayer will be stuck with the bill in the end. And in times past, the mere presence of a federal deposit insurance did not guarantee that financial corporations would thrive when risky management practices were exposed by a shaky economy. In the decade between 1979 and 1989, nearly 1,000 commercial banks failed and about half of the savings and loans went broke.[129]

The source of the problem can be traced to the organization which created the FDIC: the federal government. By the 1980s, most bank managers assumed the government would pay off their debts if they made wrong investment choices. At any one time, a failure of one or a few banking institutions would not be impossible to handle. The FDIC's risk management program would insure the banks because of the millions of taxpayers who would be responsible for the cost.

The irony behind the "guarantee" of the FDIC is that if there ever was an economic crisis in which the banking industry was damaged, and if a sizable percentage of the banks were to collapse, then the very people who would be protected, the depositors, would still be responsible for the payoff through increased taxes.[130] This is also known as self-insurance!

A report published by the U.S. Comptroller of the Currency in 1988 cautioned that a bank's aggressive corporate growth strategy would probably lead to risky investments. When the economy is moving upward, everyone is pleased with the progress, but as the market takes its regular downhill breather, the risk often becomes excessive and can push the bank backwards, sometimes to the brink of bankruptcy. The Comptroller's office advised, "If the growth takes place in a sector that is experiencing a speculative boom, [the real estate market] for example, a downturn can be sudden and severe. Overly aggressive lending under such conditions may underlie a more rapid erosion of a bank's net worth and make recovery less likely."[131]

The excessive real estate lending of the 80s caught up with the whole system. By 1991, a number of the nation's money center banks were "on the brink of insolvency." One wrong move could have broken the piggy bank held at the Bank Insurance Fund, resulting in taxpayers being responsible for a trillion dollar bill.[132]

It may be natural to expect the government to do a better job of governance, but it is not as easy as it would seem to review a bank's financial records. Watchdog agencies are regularly given the directive to audit banks to make sure they are fulfilling their fiduciary responsibility. However, the complexity of this task was exposed during the bankruptcy of the largest utility company, Enron, just ten years after FDICIA enactment, in 2001. Federal and private analysts complained that everything looked okay to them before the collapse. Even the accounting firm, Arthur Anderson, said everything was fine. But after years of mismanagement and hiding mistakes, the seventh largest corporation in America crumbled under the weight of excessive debt.[133]

In a 2001 report to a special banking subcommittee, the Comptroller again urged for action to be taken to fix the "flaws" in the program. The federal statement, written to a congressional committee, detailed moral hazard as the major problem facing the FDIC. Specifically, less risky banks were being charged an insurance premium, and in turn did "subsidize" the aggressive investments of riskier banks, "the exact opposite of what was intended by the legislation that mandated a Federal risk-based deposit insurance system."[134]

A disconcerting piece of information about the banking industry came from an economist writing for the New York Federal Reserve Board. The analyst was concerned that it is extremely difficult to financially scrutinize banks because they are so highly leveraged. Major rating firms, such as Moody's and Standard & Poor's (S&P), the very organizations which promise to give unbiased reviews of the financial industry, have a difficult time reading between the very "opaque" lines. "Uncertainty over the banks stems from their assets, loans and trading assets in particular, the risks of which are hard to observe or easy to change."[135]

Studies have found the rating firms often disagree as to the strength and solvency of these institutions. The silver lining presented by this research showed that the larger the bank, the more often the rating companies agreed. But there was still a lack of confidence in the reports since "banks' high leverage, which invites agency problems, compounds the uncertainty over their assets."[136]

But haven't we learned from the mistakes of the past? Haven't we been able to see the problems coming? Forecasting a negative view of the future, Mr. Kaufman describes the present situation:

> Unfortunately, the FDIC has not done much better than the FSLIC. Mainly due to sharp declines in commercial real estate values in the late eighties and early

> nineties, the number of commercial bank failures increased sharply from around ten annually at the beginning of the decade to more than two hundred near the end. Many large banks failed, including nine of the ten largest banks in Texas. For many of the same reasons that motivated the FSLIC, the FDIC has repeated the FSLIC's pattern. It delayed recognizing many insolvencies, particularly for large banks it considered too large to fail, denied that it was encountering financial difficulties, and increasingly resolved insolvencies at a high cost to itself and to the U.S. Treasury.[137]

In an article addressed to the Federal Reserve Board in 2000, Chris Farrell, a contributing economics editor from *Business Week* magazine, bluntly drove the point home:

> The danger haunting regulators is that the too-big-to-fail doctrine will eventually encourage reckless behavior at financial-services giants during boom times—like now. Why shouldn't management take reckless risks? After all, if the financial gambles pay off, stockholders, including option-laden executives, will pocket huge profits. But if they lose the bets when the economy tanks taxpayers will pick up the tab. This disastrous dynamic was at work during the 1980s savings-and-loan crisis.[138]

As Fed Chairman Alan Greenspan said, "The free lunch has still to be invented."[139]

The Bubble's Flux

Speak of bubbles and it is natural to look back to the stock market bubbles of the past. But there are other bubbles which may add to the overall widespread economic effect, including the pension bubble (which will be discussed in the next chapter) and the real estate bubble.

In a 2004 FDIC report, agency researchers suggested high real estate prices alone are not the chief cause of concern, rather, the worrisome mixture includes record mortgages, personal debt, and fluctuating incomes. The study says highly leveraged homeowners with volatile incomes could "face problems, even in an improving economy, leading to potentially higher loss rates in mortgage loan portfolios in the event of rising interest rates or declining local home prices."[140]

Economist George Kaufman, writing for the Federal Reserve Bank of Chicago, warned of the FDIC's potential for self-combustion. Quoting notable economists Hyman Minsky and Charles Kindleberger, Kaufman expressed the need to prepare for the damage that could be caused to the banking system by an "asset bubble," whether it was stocks or real estate.[141] A few years after his writing, the country weathered through a three year slump caused by the stock market, but the economy has not yet seen the one-two punch that could be delivered by both a real estate and stock market slide.

Kaufman detailed the possible way the banking industry could stumble:

Banks get caught up in the euphoria of budding economic expansions and expand credit rapidly to finance the increase in economic activity, [such as the 45 year low mortgage rates available in the early 2000s.] Moreover, the credit is often collateralized by the assets purchased. The credit expansion fuels and accelerates the economic expansion, accelerates asset price increases, and encourages additional speculation.

Both lenders and borrowers fall victim to 'irrational exuberance.' Through time, borrowers become more highly leveraged and turn increasingly to shorter-term debt. Their margin of safety in covering their debt service payments from operating revenues or continued increases in asset prices declines and approaches zero. Increasingly, debt servicing is financed out of new debt (in Minsky's terms-- Ponzi finance). Given the high leverage, any slight decline or even slowdown in expected revenues, no less the bursting of asset price bubbles, and even moderate increases in interest rates can cause defaults. The financial system crashes off its own weight. This leads to a self-feeding sequence of distress-selling, fire sale losses, further defaults, business failures, bank runs, and bank failures and the expansion turns into a macroeconomic downturn. Bank problems precede macroeconomic problems.[142]

No one can fault a homeowner for their desire to make lower monthly mortgage payments. The exuberant refinance craze, where millions of borrowers took advantage of historically low interest rates, could be a precursor of the defaults proposed by Kaufman.

Perhaps one of the dangers facing the FDIC will be such an implosion:

- Record low long-term mortgage interest rates of 4 to 5 percent, locked in 30 year contracts, followed by
- Soaring inflation and interest rates, not caused by a red-hot economy as in the late 1990s, but pushed up by, among other things, high medical costs and high unemployment from millions of retiring Baby Boomers, forcing
- Banks to pay out interest rates of 5 to 7 percent just to remain competitive, resulting in
- Bank failures due to more money paid out than coming in.

Looking back, economist Lawrence White says this is exactly what happened to cause the bankruptcy of the FSLIC. Unfortunately, no one in Washington could see it coming.[143]

Other economists, as noted by Kaufman, see the banking industry struggling from a nation-wide economic downturn. A financial slowdown due to a recession, could increase corporate failures and unemployment, resulting in the depletion of a bank's collateralized assets, ending in the potential of businesses defaulting on their loans or having difficulty making their loan payments.

Mr. Kaufman's parting lament:

> Finally, central banks need to act as lenders of last resort, if sudden asset price declines appear to overshoot their new lower equilibrium levels. But as central banks are unlikely to know these new levels and likely to err on the side of excessive ease, this policy could result in misallocating resources and igniting product inflation. It would be best to avoid asset price bubbles beforehand, if only we knew how![144]

Either way, whether from internal or external stress, it is a sad cycle to consider. If America wasn't depressed before, it is easy to get caught in extreme negativism now. That is why preparation is essential.

The Built-In Hazard at the FDIC

Perhaps one of the greatest risks to the American depositor comes from the federal government, probably encouraged, at one time, by some self serving lobbyist.

Imagine an insurance policy that does not require the insured to pay a dime until the risk occurs. In other words, you sign up for a fire insurance policy on your home, don't pay anything for years, and then, when you finally have a fire, you are required to make a big lump sum payment. What a deal! At least it sounds great when the incident of risk (fire, car accident, health issue, death, etc.), has not occurred. But it would be adding insult to injury to wait for the stressful incident to occur and then be required to make up for all the unpaid past expenses. Once considered, it is not such a good deal after all.

But this perversion of logic describes how banks, today, support the FDIC. For nearly 60 years, the FDIC asked banks to share payments for their insurance premiums. Every bank was equally responsible. However, since 1992 when the FDICIA was signed into law, over 9,000 financial institutions, almost 92% of the banks have been let off the hook to pay *any* insurance premiums![145] Less than 10% of America's banks make any payments, and even then they are only required to pay when their balance sheets alert the FDIC to financial problems!

Even the FDIC management is concerned this can only lead to future economic problems:

> Because of current restrictions on pricing deposit insurance, most banks and thrifts pay no insurance premiums when they are doing well, but pay high premiums when the industry is weak and banks are failing. This does not make sense for the banks or for the communities they serve. It is possible that, in difficult times, deposit insurance premiums could reduce the pre-tax net income of insured institutions by almost $9 billion. Based on current average capital and loan-to-assets ratios for all insured institutions, this reduction in income could lead to a contraction in lending of more than $65 billion at the precise time in the business cycle when loans are most needed.[146]

So, under current law, if there is a "protracted bear market" as warned by the FDIC, whether it is caused by retiring Baby Boomers or a real estate bubble, and if the ratio of assets to liabilities is decreased, the largest banks will be pushed over the edge, requiring billions of dollars of payments at the worst possible time. The FDIC appears to have been designed to be its own potential stumbling block.

The FDIC says it best:

> Banks that are paying for deposit insurance at the end of the 1990s are those that have run afoul of capital regulations or the supervisory process. This is a significant departure from past practice. Pricing of deposit insurance has evolved into a penalty system for the few, rather than a priced service for all.
>
> Thus, a decade that began with a legislative mandate for risk-based insurance premiums ended with the FDIC providing a free guarantee of almost three trillion dollars in bank and thrift liabilities. As a result, the moral hazard problems FDICIA intended to address with risk-based deposit insurance may have become more firmly entrenched than ever.[147]

The FDIC quarterly report shows banks, savings institutions, and credit unions are not so "safe and secure." First, 47% of all deposits held by FDIC guaranteed banks are <u>not</u> insured. Digging further into the national statistics, banks state that nearly 75% of their assets are assigned to Fannie Mae,

Freddie Mac, and Ginnie Mae backed mortgage or business loans, almost all of it attached to real estate. Only 5% of the assets are cash. In other words, if real estate values decline, so will the assets held by banks.[148] If assets drop because of a falling real estate market, then the banks' underlying investments will be weakened resulting in possible bankruptcies.

How do American taxpayers get themselves out of this one?

The Un-Agency

The financial and banking world as we knew it changed dramatically after the bankruptcy of the FSLIC and the actions of Congress in 1991 and 1996 (the Federal Deposit Insurance Corporation Improvement Act and the Deposit Insurance Funds Act). In fact, Mr. Kaufman says there is no "fund" as the majority of American's assume,[149] and the safety net guarantee is not what it was at one time:[150]

> It is no longer totally accurate to describe insured deposits at banks as 'federally insured.' The resources of the banking industry stand behind the FDIC. The deposit insurance law does retain language that appears to suggest a continued federal government obligation. For example, the 1989 Financial Institutions Reform, Recovery and Enforcement Act (FIRREA) requires each insured bank to display "a statement that insured deposits are backed by the full faith and credit of the United States

> Government." That language, which preceded the FDICIA reforms, is not by itself a full faith and credit guarantee of insured deposits; at most, it creates a moral obligation of the federal government.
>
> As a practical matter, the obligation would exist anyway, because it is not conceivable that the federal government would permit insured depositors to suffer losses in a government-sponsored deposit insurance scheme. However, after FDICIA, the federal government has no obligation to make any payments to insured depositors unless and until the resources of the banking industry as a whole are fully exhausted. Further, the government has no obligation— moral or otherwise—to make payments to uninsured depositors or other creditors.[151]

The end product is the protection everyone assumes they are getting is much different than what they once had. The federal government is not the primary source of protection for savings and checking accounts. The FDIC has become more of a real estate broker, selling off assets of failing banks to other institutions. Banks are the first line of defense, followed by the promised government support.

Although some economists take the pessimistic route, most seem to be optimists who stress the point that America will probably never allow the FDIC to fail. However, what the public can't control is the amount of taxes that may have to be shoveled in to salvage the system in the event of a financial collapse. If the real estate and the stock markets should ever crash at the same time, the FDIC, and specifically the U.S. Government, will be pushed to its limit as taxes could skyrocket to take care of the huge debt. Or, as some predict, the FDIC may have to take the same road the FSLIC took and go bankrupt.

The mere discussion of the potential failure of the FDIC does not mean that depositors will immediately lose their deposited money. It does imply, however, that bank failures easily could cause the FDIC to need an influx of federal funds to pay for the guarantees, which means, increased taxes. The unemotional answer of "So what!" from those who are only looking out for their own money, can be answered with a "Just wait!" Someone will pay, and it will be the FDIC-protected depositor, also known as the taxpayer.

If this worse case scenario unfolds, taxes may soar, and inflation may be uncontrollable.

Preparation is the key.

09:00

The FDIC's "Perfect Storm"

What happens when one in five people retire? Are you set? What happens when the real estate market slows? Will you be affected? What happens when the economy hits a recession? Are you Prepared? What happens when companies can't pay pensions?

Wait a minute. First Medicare, then Social Security, and now America has to worry about pensions?

Reduced Retirement? Penniless Pensions? But that's not fair! Retirees have worked all their lives expecting retirement funds to be available upon demand. They say, "It can't be!"

But according to the government, pensions may be the next "perfect storm."[152]

Through the turn of the millennium, most hopeful retirees have assumed the companies they grew old with will continue to be strong, and if not, then the federal government will be there to protect their retirement checks. These "pensions" do not include individual IRAs, 401(k)s, or 403(b)s. They are specifically those funds left with employers which promise to pay a retirement based on the years of employment, pay scale, actuarial tables, and percentage of participation, among other things.

Up to now, the federal government has guaranteed the retirement money of pensioners. Similar to the FDIC's mandate, the Pension Benefit Guaranty Corporation (PBGC) was created to protect retirement benefits under ERISA (Employee Retirement Income Security Act of 1974). More than 32,000 pension plans are insured by the PBGC, amounting to about one and a half trillion dollars in 2004.

There's trouble brewing, though, when, in 2004, 77 million retirees are expecting their retirement to be safe and secure, but in reality, the government *corporation,* designed to protect their money is underfunded by nearly 25%!

The FDIC is concerned about the potential problem:

> Declining stock valuations, a sustained period of low interest rates, structural changes in the workplace, and a regulatory and accounting structure in need of reform have coalesced into a "***perfect storm***" for U.S. corporate defined benefit pension plans. Even though the stock market recently has rebounded, the Pension Benefit Guaranty Corporation (PBGC) estimates that U.S. pensions in defined benefit plans were underfunded by more than $350 billion as of September

> 15, 2003.... The PBGC['s] cushion to protect these plans has eroded. The value of the agency's single employer insurance program declined dramatically from a $9.7 billion surplus in 2000 to an estimated $8.8 billion deficit in August 2003 (see Chart 1 below).[153] (Italics added, Chart printed from FDIC report)

The 2004 "Performance and Accountability Report" shows the PBGC was hit by the largest loss in the history of the program. The result is that more than a million retirees have underfunded pensions of nearly a half a trillion dollars ($450 billion) or a 22% drop from the year before.[154]

Analysts for the PBGC reported in 2004[155] that a number of factors resulted in the "erosion" of the federal guaranty fund:

- The U.S. government assumed the loss of a number of large plans,
- The decline of the stock market had negative effects on the valuations of defined benefit pensions, and
- The low interest rates required to lift the economy out of its recession and subsequent doldrums increased pension liabilities.

PBGC administrators warn this current crisis will take 12 years of premiums to pull out of the tail spin it is in. The report cautions there will be unforeseen results on the banks and the FDIC, as well. "Defined benefit pension problems can affect the competitiveness and cash flow of sponsoring companies, some of which borrow from FDIC-insured institutions."[156] The unanswered question remains: What happens in the event of another sharp economic downturn within this period of time?

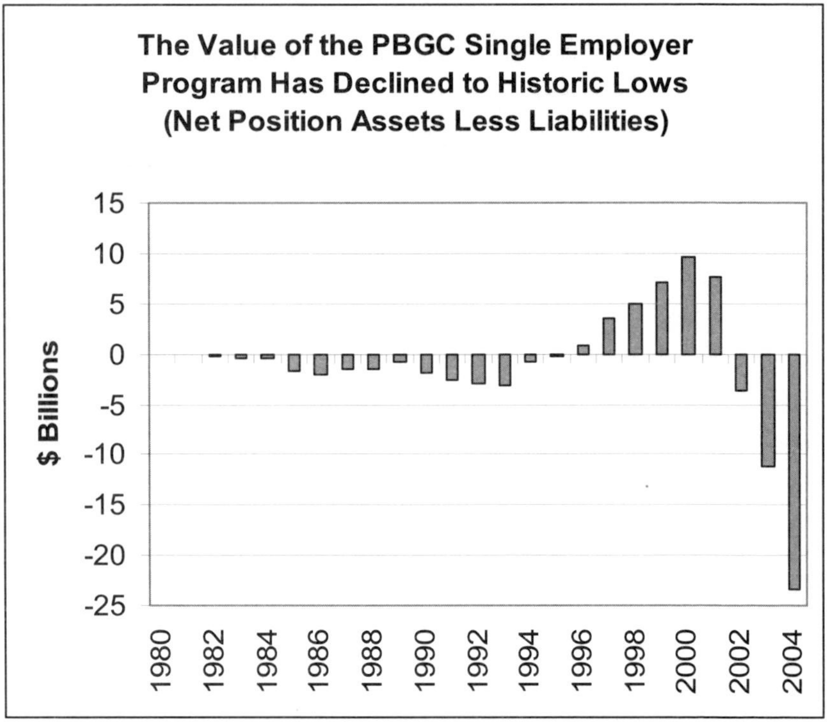

Source: Pension Benefit Guaranty Corporation, November 2004

The failure of one huge institutionalized pension plan may wreak havoc with the federally protected banks. The director of the PBGC worries 80 percent of the workforce that does not have pensions may be required to pay for the 20 percent of the country who are "protected" pensioners through a bail-out by taxpayers.[157]

The Death Knell?

From the FDIC report, "An Update on Emerging Issues in Banking," the potential collapse of the PBGC could only make things worse and be one more falling domino adding to a potential major crisis for the economy. This report, dated January 13, 2004, details the "magnitude of the problem":

> According to data provided in a Federal Reserve study, all U.S. pension plans lost an estimated $1 trillion during the recent downturn in the stock market. Even so, pensions are an important part of the household asset mix....
>
> As a result of defined benefit pension fund asset erosion, several firms have terminated their plans, and many others have become significantly underfunded. The Federal Reserve study found that 353 of the S&P 500 corporations had defined benefit pensions at year-end 2002; *ninety-one percent of these plans were underfunded* by an aggregate $222 billion. Moreover, defined benefit plans sponsored by several large corporations – for example, Delta Airlines, Goodyear Tire, General Motors (GM), and McDermit International – at one time reported funding gaps in excess of their 2002 market capitalization.
>
> The PBGC sustained the largest one-year financial loss in its 28-year history in 2002, primarily due to record losses from

> completed and probable plan terminations.... By the end of fiscal year 2003, the amount of defined benefit plan underfunding in financially troubled companies could more than double, possibly exceeding $80 billion....[158] (Italics added.)

American auto makers, steel workers, and transportation employees are going to feel the cash crunch the most. To put the problem into perspective, Chrysler, Ford, and General Motors include $631 to $1,360 in the price of every new car just to pay for pensions. Large amounts of bonds have been sold; however, GM, for example, has been losing ground, paying out 7.54 percent bond interest rates, requiring 9 percent to break even, but coming up short on their investments.[159]

Local economies throughout the United States could feel the pension pinch through a "ripple effect". The FDIC report cautions its member banks to prepare for repercussions in the future if the PBGC has to "seize plans" due to poor performance.[160] Those areas of the country which could be negatively affected would be states such as Arizona or Florida, with high concentrations of retirees, or those states with large numbers of old-line industries, such as auto, metal and transportation workers.

One example in November 2003, which provides a look into future troubles, was reported in the Chicago Tribune. When employees from Bethlehem Steel went to take their early retirement, they were dismayed when they found their pensions slashed by 40%, from up to an expected $30,000 a year to less than

$18,000. That kind of lifestyle change will affect retirees purchases from real estate to durable goods to travel plans.[161]

Attempting to plan for the future, Steven Kandarian, then director of the PBGC in 2003, said, "in a worst-case scenario, the PBGC could take on so many claims from underfunded pension plans that a taxpayer bailout could be the only recourse. This could weaken public confidence in pension funds and constrain consumer and business spending [resulting in a possible recession]. If companies were required to immediately re-fund pension shortfalls, cash flows would be directed away from capital investment, expansion, and debt service. Old-line industries would be particularly hard hit, and the global competitiveness of these companies undoubtedly would suffer. In this scenario, the FDIC would expect that corporate credit quality would be affected."[162]

Big corporations take out huge loans. Financial institutions invest in corporate bonds. The PBGC is funded by Treasury Bonds which goes to invest in federally funded mortgages. The FDIC and the rest of the government sponsored enterprises will feel the impact if the foundation of any of these organizations are shocked by a major economic crisis.

As of 2004, the nation's pension program, including social security, according to director Bradley B. Belt, is "extraordinarily underfunded" and will only get worse. The "flaws with the design of the pension insurance system lead to a massive 'moral hazard' problem. To be sure, any insurance system runs the risk of encouraging "bad" behavior, but the level of moral hazard plaguing the pension insurance system is staggering."

The PBGC director continues, "Has the death knell sounded for defined benefit plans and the PBGC? If we do nothing, I fear that the trend lines... will not only continue but accelerate, and the defined benefit pension plan will be consigned to the dustbin of history.... However, I do not believe these outcomes are a foregone conclusion. On the contrary, with timely intervention, I believe we can prevent the problems of today from becoming the crisis of tomorrow."[163]

On Collision Course or a Near-Miss?

The PBGC is only one of more than a dozen government agencies designed to protect and guarantee the public's savings accounts, mortgages, pensions, as well as most of America's business, farm, and student loans.

In his June 2003 opening remarks before a congressional subcommittee reviewing the Government Subsidized Enterprises (GSEs), Chairman Richard Baker (R-Louisiana), gave the following warning and observation:

> When a GSE fails, it will quickly fall through its limited capital, right through the shareholders, directly to the taxpayer.... I began my remarks this morning revisiting the events of June 15, 2002, the day Arthur Anderson was found guilty of obstruction of justice by a Texas court. Another historic event occurred just

> 24 hours earlier on June 14, 2002, not receiving near as much attention. An object known as 2002 NM passed within 75,000 miles of Earth, to be known in astronomical terms as a "near miss." How close is that really? Well, the moon is about 137,000 miles away. So this object passed inside the orbit of the moon. As far as we know, this was the second closest near miss in human history.
>
> So what else is significant about this event? Well, how about this fact: Scientists on earth did not know about 2002 NM ***until three days after its passage***. How is this possible in this world of scientific technological sophistication? The answer is simple. We don't have enough resources committed or enough people watching to assure against a clearly cataclysmic event from occurring...The parallel is clear. Unless we act to enhance our supervisory capacity of the two housing GSEs that Congress has created, [Fannie Mae and Freddie Mac], we may not see the next systemic event coming until it is too late.[164] (Italics and bold added)

Meanwhile, the economic time bomb continues to tick, waiting for the suggested answers to work. If the system isn't quickly fixed, the one place where the economic dominos will start to tumble may be America's huge retirement-disaster-in-the-making, sponsored by the Pension Benefit Guaranty Corporation.

Is it already "too late?" Is this something that should have been recognized decades ago? As noted in the previous chapter, at least one economist has criticized that the American government's economic system may be more accurately described as a "Ponzi Scheme," living off the incomes of future generations, where someone will eventually pay.

10:00

Our Unstable World

"The sky is falling," cried Chicken Little.

No, as learned from the centuries old fable, the sky was not falling. But the moral of the story was this little chicken, at the first sign of trouble, could only assume the negative and, depending on who told the tale, usually ended up in trouble with the big bad Foxy Loxy.

Now, readers should not be too harsh about Chicken Little's hasty conclusion. Anything is possible. Whether it's the ever changing weather, satellites breaking up on re-entry, crashing planes, colliding meteors or asteroids, collapsing government agencies, or even plummeting stock prices, the investing public should at least be aware of the possibility that something *could* happen out of the ordinary, especially in a world where we are uncertain what is around the next corner.

For some people it is easy to be pessimistic about the future of the economy. They are called the "Bears," or "Contrarians," always assuming the stock market will go down into hibernation. Other investors, expressing unbridled optimism, dubbed the "Bulls," charge ahead expecting the economy button to be stuck on Growth. Meanwhile, most investors probably vacillate somewhere between.

Even with all the evidence pointing to troubles ahead, there is no need to fear when adequately prepared. Now, it is impossible to be ready for everything, but there are indicators showing up in the world's economy that are flashing warning signs of impending financial danger. Although the average investor may not be able to change the flow of the worldwide economy, there may be some benefit derived from at least being alerted to the trouble, even if the end result is nothing more than being set for the worst case scenario.

So far, it appears the scenes have been scripted and the drama is preparing to unfold. The main players are the government and the public, soon to be acted upon by unemployment, inflation, and the stock and real estate markets. Although moral hazard is one of the key struggles in this play, there are a number of other influences which may hasten the impending crisis.

Terrorism: The World at War

Ever since September 11, 2001, Americans have looked upwards when a plane flies overhead, as a tinge of anxiety still remains from that sad day when extremists crashed four huge airliners killing thousands. For years after, the fear of terrorism has tugged on the stock market and resulted in a less than enthusiastic view of the world's financial future. The mood on Wall Street is definitely somber compared to the "irrational exuberance" of the 1990s.

For more than a dozen years after the official close of the Cold War, the United States was lulled into assuming the destruction of 9/11 would only happen somewhere "over there." Now, the world's economy is more sensitive to the repercussions of anarchy, war, or other types of political uncertainties in the most remote parts of the world. It was not long ago when a bomb threat in the news was ignored by Wall Street. Now the market drops if corn starch is mailed in a white envelope as authorities expect anthrax or some other potential bio-terrorism.

Some ask in disbelief, what happened to make the world so unstable? Probably nothing. The current events of the world seem more volatile for one simple fact: information is more readily available from multiple sources than in the past. The ready availability of cable, satellite, and internet news reports has allowed the "good guys," the "bad guys," and the "spectators" to have instant access to information which speeds up results, strategic countermoves, and encourages unstable copycats.

The alarm was sounded on February 23, 1998, by Osama bin Laden as he declared a Jihad, or "Holy War" against America and its citizens.[165] In response, Islamic leaders from around the world denounced the call to kill all Americans,[166] but unfortunately, that has not deterred the intense hatred from continuing to build.

In a speech delivered twelve days before the World Trade Center attack, Indian author and Nobel Prize winner V.S. Naipaul explained such radical values were based on Nihilism, "the belief that destruction of existing political or social institutions is necessary for future improvement." [167] The Russians saw a similar movement begin in the 1800s. Just as the Aryan Nation or Nazism can trace their extremist ideologies to religion, Naipaul cautioned that the world's enemy is not Islam; it is fanatical groups, such as Al Qaeda, which are so dangerous to the rest of humanity.

Quoting Naipaul, George Krauthammer, editorialized in the New York Post:

> "We are within reach of great nihilistic forces that have undone civilization." In places like Afghanistan, "religion has been turned by some into a kind of nihilism, where people wish to destroy themselves and destroy their past and their culture... to be pure. They are enraged about the world and they wish to pull it down.' This kind of fury and fanaticism is unappeasable. It knows no social, economic, or political solution. 'You cannot converge with this [position] because it holds that your life is worthless and your beliefs are criminal and should be extirpated"....
>
> Once again, the world is faced with a transcendent conflict between those who love life and those who love death both for themselves and their enemies. Which is why we tremble....

> We tremble because for the first time in history, nihilism will soon be armed with the ultimate weapons of annihilation. For the first time in history, the nihilist will have the means to match his ends. Which is why the war declared upon us on September 11 is the most urgent not only of our lives, but in the life of civilization itself.[168]

Unfortunately, America learned, shockingly too late, the modern terrorist is more educated and able to take advantage of up-to-date technology to deploy their weapons of destruction. This is why preparation has become so vital. Today, as never before, the terrorist has the means to follow through on their extreme threats, whether via jumbo jetliners used as huge gas filled bombs or through other methods like "dirty bombs," small nuclear devices able to be discreetly carried in briefcases.

Life in the future will be different than the Cold War of the past, as these international guerrillas are eager to act out their plans. Whereas the giant Soviet Union was held in check by the counter threat of the United States, terrorists hide among the innocent, making it difficult for security forces to root them out.

While America must continue to improve international diplomacy and be vigilant to guard against outside threats, a warning voice must be sounded to its citizens to watch for guerrilla tactics on this country's shores.

If terrorism was the only concern, government leaders could devote all their efforts attempting to protect the public against attack. But there are so many imminent dangers to the fragile national economy; issues such as illegal immigration, drug smuggling, corporate white-collar crime, oil shortages. Now, other trials may be looming, such as potential economic disasters congress has little control over.

The Health Care Emergency

When it comes to paying for health care, as one consultant asks, "How far do you go?"[169]

Consider the situations: A loved one is battling cancer, or some other deadly disease, how much health care is enough? A two-pound premature baby struggling to hold on to life deserves all the care possible, but who pays the $700,000 medical bill?

In these instances, quality insurance is invaluable, but as Dr. Seth Garber suggests, the more health care is used, the more expensive it becomes. "For example, you're not just paying for the cost of a heart bypass, but the fact that many, many people, including 80-year-olds, are having them. Add to this the fact that between the ages of 45 and 65, a person's use of health care will triple. By the year 2030, we'll have twice as many people over 65. Then, when you hit 80, you use nine times the health care services. And guess what? We're living longer."

Meanwhile, the cost to keep the American health care industry alive has reached crisis proportions, and appears to be getting worse. Currently 20% of the federal budget is going to pay for health care[170] for federal employees and vets, Medicare and Medicaid recipients, Community Health Centers and other services. The government expects this cost to escalate beyond control in the next few decades.

To put the cost of insurance into perspective, General Motors spends more to provide health care coverage for its 1.1 million insured workers and retirees than it does to buy steel each year! In 2003, that amounted to more than $4.8 billion dollars. With health care inflation costs at 12% per year, the automaker is expecting costs to more than double in 6 years.[171] Currently there are 500,000 retirees who look to GM to take care of their future pensions and health care and that number will only go up.

On the national level, as Baby Boomers start early retirement as soon as 2008, health care costs are expected to skyrocket to take care of the 77 million new retirees. The government anticipates Medicare to go bankrupt by 2019.[172] The crisis will spill over into every facet of the economy as taxpayers will be hit with a huge tax hike.

Legal malpractice costs are driving the health care industry out of business. A recent government study shows 76% of the doctors believe malpractice lawsuits have hurt the quality of care they would normally provide their patients and nearly 80% of the doctors ordered additional tests or referred patients to specialists out of fear they could face legal trouble or have their malpractice insurance premiums increased.[173]

The report confirms health care insurance increased 505% in 25 years through 2001. Doctors and hospitals are facing the same frustrating rise in costs.

In fact, doctors are quitting their once lucrative practices, hospitals are being driven out of business, and some parts of the country are losing medical care altogether, mainly because of rising insurance and legal expenses.[174]

The Health Care Crisis is not going to go away, and it could traumatize an already weakened economy.

Population Implosion: Economic Implosion?

Over the past fifty years the world has experienced extraordinary progress in medicine, food production, and many other advances leading to a longer and higher quality life. At the same time, a major change in "traditional" values created a shift in how people view the family and the number of children desired in the "ideal" family unit. The combination of a longer life and fewer children may soon result in a financial crisis that may only be satisfied by significantly increased immigration, considered an undesirable consequence by some forecasters.

Looking back, zero population advocates may not have realized their dream could turn into their own economic nightmare. From a financial standpoint, there will be too many elderly and not enough young people to replace them. Statistically the trend is nearing a disaster.[175]

As people live longer, the level of fertility among women throughout the world has decreased more than 20% in 12 years. The United States Census Bureau projections released in March of 2004 suggest the fertility rate for the world will drop below replacement level before 2050.[176]

Predicting the future outcome of the national demographic shift is very tricky, as there are trade-offs on either side of the issue. Assuming the Census Bureau reports are correct, the overpopulation concern may taper off over time. Still, fears of food, water and oil shortages may continue. However, a whole new set of questions may rear up, such as addressing healthcare costs, caring for millions of needy elderly, troubles replacing the retirees in the labor pool, and the tax burden citizens of the future will be required to carry.

The Census Bureau reports, "The population of labor force age is expected to grow steadily while its proportion of the total stays approximately the same. The world's elderly population, on the other hand, is projected to grow considerably in both absolute and relative terms. The elderly are projected to be more than three times as many in 2050 as [in 2002], and comprise nearly 17% of global population compared with 7% in 2002."[177]

Alan Greenspan, at a Federal Reserve Symposium held in August 2004 suggested there were few viable options. He suggested the Baby Boomers should reconsider early retirement. It is apparent the Fed chairman may attempt to push the retirement age set by Chancellor Bismarck to a more mature time of life. "To date... despite the improving feasibility of work at older ages, Americans have been retiring at younger ages. But rising pressures on retirement incomes and a growing scarcity of experienced labor could eventually reverse that trend."[178]

There was a time when the gray haired greeter at Walmart was one of those retirees who wanted to have something to do. It was a wonderful way to stay busy, and provide some service to the community. Could gray hair soon be the norm behind the counter at the hamburger stand, the local grocery store, even pizza delivery? The retirees of the future may be working out of necessity just to make ends meet.

The alert was sounded again by Mr. Greenspan:

> The changes projected for the United States are not as dramatic as those projected for other areas--particularly Europe and Japan--but they nonetheless present substantial challenges. The growth rate of the working-age population in the United States is anticipated to slow from about 1 percent per year today to about 1/4 percent per year by 2035. At the same time, the percentage of the population that is over 65 is poised to rise markedly--from about 12 percent today to perhaps 20 percent by 2035...

But according to the Census Bureau, this will only happen if new immigrants pick up the slack. [179] Greenspan continued his assessment in 2004:

> The growth rate of the U.S. working-age population is expected to decline substantially over the next two decades and to remain low thereafter. But the fraction of that population that is employed will almost surely be affected by changes in the economic returns to

> working and especially for older workers, improvements in health.[180]

At the same time the Fed chairman recommends increased immigration as the answer, he warns "immigration would have to be much larger than almost all current projections assume." [181]

Meanwhile, many want to slow down the super highway of legal and illegal immigrants coming into the United States. The political action committees want to keep the number to what it was in the 50s and 60s, somewhere around a quarter to a third of a million, rather than the current one million immigrants.[182] Following Mr. Greenspan's recommend-dations, some activists say the U.S. Census Bureau's projection of 400 million people is sure to be reached with negative implications. "The more the population grows, the less livable our country is likely to become....[due to] population crowding, urban sprawl, diminishing rural and wilderness lands, traffic gridlock, and resource limits such as the energy crisis in California."[183]

The anti-immigration groups point to statistics which show the average immigrant is not educated, with only a ninth-grade education, and only six percent are admitted on the basis of their skills. "Because immigrants' English proficiency is lower than Americans', their children often require special education to compensate. At a time when our schools are struggling to properly educate the children we already have, immigration is making the job much harder."[184]

In addition, the Census Bureau predicts that a high number of immigrants are coming to this country to take advantage of the elder care benefits, and by 2100, the number of elderly who were immigrants, will be as high as 13 percent, and double the number in 2000.[185]

However, looking at the other side of the argument, without lower paid entry level workers, many of whom may possibly be immigrants, the excessive cost of long term care may bankrupt society.

Which is it going to be: millions of welfare dependent immigrants, or millions of welfare dependent elderly?

The situation brings a new twist to the Statue of Liberty proclamation, "Give me your tired, your poor, your huddled masses yearning to breathe free...."[186]

Someday soon Congress must make a decision that will be unpopular with someone.

Meanwhile, Paul Hewitt, of the Social Security Administration, conjectured how the aging time bomb could eventually affect the world: "It's going to be extremely hard for businesses to make a profit. And when businesses don't make a profit, they don't pay taxes. And when taxes don't get paid, you can't support the welfare state. And so the older countries face such a huge problem financially that they really could undermine the global economy."[187]

Many elderly, with no children, will be left without families. The obvious result will be the increasing elderly population who will be on their own. With no family to support them, the state will be left to care for millions of elderly, adding to the burden placed on the taxpayer.

As Fed Chairman Greenspan and other economists have stated, we can not predict what will happen. We have never had a world economy locked in such a way to an extremely unstable political and socio-economic environment.

And talking about the environment…

Empty Swimming Pools:
A Drought Like We've Never Seen

First, what does the weather have to do with the economy? The short answer: No drinkable water, no civilization. No irrigation water for the great plains, the "Bread Basket" of America, no bread.

Second, when discussing the weather, there is one essential point that needs to be stressed. No one knows what will happen next. Weathercasters have a general rule of thumb that there is an 80% chance of getting their prediction right for the first 24 hours. The probability drops to 20% accuracy for the next two to five days, and after that, it's anybody's guess.

But the reason this is such an essential topic, is that climatologists, those scientists who study weather history, ancient lake beds and tree rings, warn that during this century our weather may possibly revert to the old pattern, namely, long decades of drought.

Looking back, one western realtor said, "While growing up in the 1950s, my father told me we were running out of water. Well, that didn't happen. We will always have enough. There will always be enough water to take care of us. You'll see."

Yes, the drought of the 1950s was a replay of the 1930s "Dust Bowl," especially for people in the West. And historically, from a climatologist's point of view, the 20th century was one of the wettest on record.[188] The period from the early 1960s to 1998 provided prime "wet" weather and encouraged millions of retirees to trek south and west to the warmer sunshine states. The state of Arizona, alone, grew 585% in those fifty years.[189] Since 1950, California's population tripled. One out of eight people in the United States have come to live in California, half of which are dependent on one source of water, the Colorado River.[190]

However, the weather pattern is expected to return to a much drier cycle leaving the next hundred years with the possibility of a number of long droughts.[191]

Add to this the fact that since 1999, "the Interior West is drier now than it was during the catastrophic Dust Bowl drought of the 1930s, the worst of the 20th Century, when crops failed across the Great Plains and farm families fled by the thousands."[192] The weather, from 1999 to 2004 was officially the driest in the 98 years that the U.S. Geological Survey began keeping records.[193] Meanwhile, according to scientists, the first drought of the 21st Century may last for a number of years, even with a weak El Niño expected to bring a brief respite.[194]

The Colorado River Basin, which feeds many of the states west of the Mississippi River, has had its annual water flow drop more than 50% in the past hundred years. An El Niño weather pattern can return at any time to the Pacific Coast, but reviewing past climate cycles, it appears the amount of rain has not been enough to offset the dry years.

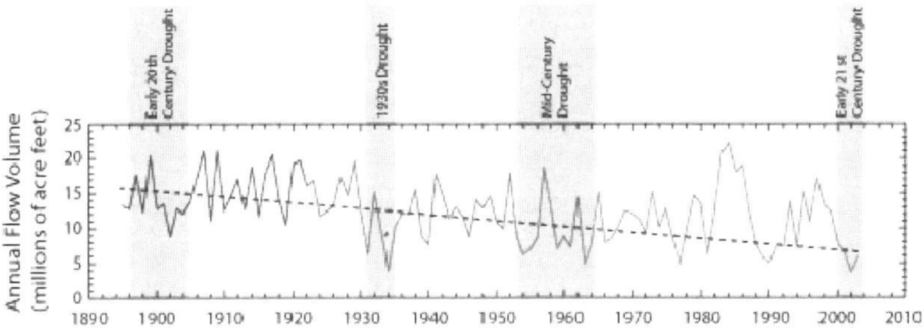

Time-series plot of the annual flow volume (in millions of acre-feet) for the Colorado River at Lee's Ferry. Dashed line is the linear trend for the period. Vertical bars and shading delineate drought periods as defined using the Palmer Drought Severity Index for the climate divisions encompassing the upper Colorado River basin.
U.S. Geological Survey, USGS Fact Sheet 2004-3062, version 2, August 2004

The challenge to urban developers is to identify how to provide more water for an influx of retirees at a time when the water flow has been on the decline. In the past, some major droughts in the west have lasted more than 20 years at a time.[195]

The lack of water is not the only issue when it comes to having enough to irrigate crops, drink, or fill swimming pools. Lake Powell, once America's second largest reservoir, located on the Colorado River bordering Arizona and Utah, has lost so much water, that hydrologists say by 2007, it will not be able to generate electricity through its huge turbines. It will take 15 years of normal precipitation to return to the level it once was.[196]

The western drought is starting to shut down farmers and ranchers and "threatens power shortages and price spikes... as anemic flows curtail hydroelectricity generation in the Pacific Northwest."[197]

One scientific journal suggests there will continue to be a dramatic rise in summer heat with depleted mountain snow packs. Scientists say Los Angeles, under the most optimistic computer model, will see heat waves increase fourfold, decreasing the Sierra Nevada snow pack up to 70 percent.[198]

The report suggests the California economy will be hurt in a number of areas. Throughout the west drinking and irrigation water for agriculture will be affected as three out of four models predict rainfall to be up to 30% less than normal.

The travel industry will be affected as skiers will not have as much snow as in the past. Because spring will come earlier, there will be more chances of flooding. California will rely more on scarce ground-water, even at a time that the drought and heat wave increases. Wildfires will be more prevalent.

What about the rest of the United States? During the worst of the 1930s drought, 80% of the U.S. was affected. But drought is not the only potential climatic disaster that may affect the economy.[199]

The National Geographic magazine for September 2004, added the following stunning article and subtitles: [200]

"Signs from Earth:

• Carbon Dioxide Levels Rise • Mercury Climbs • Oceans Warm • Glaciers Melt • Sea Level Rises • Sea Ice Thins • Permafrost Thaws • Wildfires Increase • Lakes Shrink • Lakes Freeze Up Later • Ice Shelves Collapse • Droughts Linger • Precipitation Increases • Mountain Streams Run Dry • Winter Loses Its Bite • Spring Arrives Earlier • Autumn Comes Later • Plants Flower Sooner • Migration Times Vary • Habitats Change • Birds Nest Earlier • Diseases Spread • Coral Reefs Bleach • Snow Peaks Decline • Exotic Species Invade • Amphibians Disappear • Coastlines Erode • Cloud Forests Dry • Temperatures Spike at High Altitudes

What in the World is Going On?"

As the article states, these are not future fear-driven headlines, these conditions are happening right now.

What does this mean for the United States? What are the ramifications for the rest of the economy? Could this be another ingredient in the perfect storm which may come at the wrong time?

11:00

There Is Nothing To Fear But ...

What are you afraid of? Snakes? Bugs? Heights?

How about *Old* People?

Rather than fearing fear, as FDR said, in the near future we may lament, "There is nothing to fear... but ourselves."

Growing old, as they say, is not for sissies. It can be downright scary. Some day, years in the future, when we are long gone, there may come a time when cynical historians will look back at the age of the "beautiful people," when everyone was young and successful and had lots of money and hair. That, will say the disparager, was before everyone got old and began retiring and started to suck up all the spare money to hang on to life as long as they could.

So, if you were an economist in the early 2000s, your greatest fear would best be described as instability. Your ideal economy, your dream, would be the hope to have everyone physically and fiscally happy, to be healthy and to maximize financial production at the same time positioning interest rates to promote economic stability.[201] You would want the people of the world to always have the opportunity to make more money and to keep prices steady. Perhaps among your greatest financial worries, would be uncontrollable runaway inflation or its wicked counterpart, deflation, because either one would cause a recession or worse yet, a large depression resulting in the stagnation of the economy and the potential collapse of the stock market.

Looking forward to the real world of America's future, a depression may result if millions of people retire then vote to avoid decreased benefits, increased taxes and immigration. At least this is what many economists are nervous about.[202] This scenario could cause runaway inflation because Congress will need to find a source of income from somewhere. So, out of necessity, the House and Senate will probably increase taxes on the backs of corporations which will, in turn increase prices anyway. That's inflation.

From Boom to Bust

Economist Dr. Bob Goodman expects the human wave of retiring workers will cause the stock market to retract following the decreasing workforce. [203] Real estate may follow. Taxes and inflation could increase. There will be more outstretched hands than ever before waiting for what they "deserve" because of self-serving political promises. Part of the reason will be a need to increase immigration to bring in more low paid, poorly educated elder-care assistants. Millions of the nurses aides, required to take care of millions of elderly, will be eligible for financial assistance. The medical industry and healthcare for most Americans will continue to improve resulting in longer lives.

This is the *real* time bomb bringing on potentially the longest depression in modern America. This will be nothing more than that perfect economic storm the theorists, economists and analysts have been expecting. Multiple recessions coupled with stagnation causing a prolonged Bear Market. This is a period of time in which the stock market can potentially plummet thirty to fifty per cent or more.

Unfortunately there will be few places to hide. Even the FDIC has warned their "guarantee" will not be able to anchor down the economy if the going gets too rough and all the elements meet at the same time:

- Fertility rates are declining worldwide
- Health care and longevity of life are improving
- People are living longer than ever before
- Medical costs are skyrocketing
- More than 77 million Baby Boomers will retire in two decades
- Social Security and Medicaid may go bankrupt
- A decrease in qualified labor and an increase in retirees will result in a decrease of taxable income to the government
- As the tax base decreases government may be required to increase corporate taxes
- Corporations possibly will pass the increased expenses to the consumer which may result in inflation
- The stock market could respond negatively

- A prolonged bear market can weaken corporate structure decreasing the quality rating of bonds
- The FDIC warns that a prolonged bear market could cause its bankruptcy and the of the banking guarantee
- The PBGC has a perfect storm of its own as retirees learn their pensions are no longer available
- An unprecedented depression could ensue
- Real estate, as a lagging economy, may suffer as interest rates rise to cut back inflation
- Deflation or stagnation could possibly result
- Excessive corporate and consumer debt would add to the economic downfall
- International unrest or war may follow
- Terrorists may see their opportune moment to further weaken the unsteady economy

Finally, the long-term financial life-cycles are catching up with us.

Which Way to Go?

The economy can be described as a freight train on a long climb up and over the mountains. The engineer and brakeman (the Federal Reserve Board) must always be on guard to have the engine and brakes in top condition. They don't want to get part way up a mountain side to stall with no where to go but to perilously roll backwards. At the opposite extreme, when the engine is chugging along and the train finally makes it to the top of the next big summit, the brakeman needs to be confident the brakes will hold, once again, wanting to avoid a runaway train from possible derailment. When the brakes start to show signs of wear it's up to the brakeman to come up with a solution. It is an unenviable position. If the brakes work everyone says, "No big deal. It was his job." If the brakes should ever fail, the armchair conductors would immediately call to have the brakeman replaced, saying the brakeman should have seen it coming and tried to get the problem fixed.

In the case of the economy, the Federal Reserve Board, Social Security Administration, and Congress have all waited for Mr. and Mrs. Public to express sufficient concern to stop the economic train long enough to fix the problem. But the public, at least up through the first decade of the 2000s does not want to be inconvenienced. Now, it appears the brakes may be so worn that no amount of braking will be able to control the financial instability that may potentially derail the world's economy.

If forecasters are already aware of the looming crisis, if our federal and state politicians have the ability to anticipate the negative ingredients of this potential perfect storm, then what is the problem? Why doesn't someone just go out and do something about it?

In a special report to Congress, describing how to derail a recession, government analysts have stated that "Our knowledge of the economy simply remains – and will probably always remain – too limited to 'see the problem coming.'"[204]

However, with the impending retirement of 77 million Baby Boomers, that excuse isn't true. The potential economic catastrophe has been apparent for years. No one has been willing to do anything about it. Certain analysts would prefer to say "where did that come from?"

Being Cautious May Be Bad for the Economy

For years financial advisors have taught their clients that while they are employed they can take an aggressive approach to their investments. However, when they retire, they are encouraged to be more cautious by switching to a predominant income style of investing. This means moving their portfolio from a heavy dosage of stock funds to accounts primarily holding bond and cash funds.

This careful and prudent style of investing could cause the stock market to flatten out for years and even drop into recession as a prolonged bear market.

For illustration purposes, let's assume that the 77 million retiring investors decide to switch their investment style from their 80% stock/20% bond diversified portfolio to a more conservative 20% stock/ 80% bond portfolio.

What could happen to the market if tens of millions of new retirees responded to the negative predictions of the future within a short period of time? If one in three investors on Wall Street decided to be cautious for a 20 year period and dumped their stocks for "safer" bonds there would be a major drop in the stock market averages.

To demonstrate how this could happen, take a look at the following simplified chart representing a portfolio held by a retiring investor.

	Stocks	Bonds
Before Retirement	80%	20%
After Retirement	20%	80%
Difference	-60%	+60%

These fictional investors could affect the stock market by selling out 60% of their stock. As the retirees sell, there is the potential that the working investors may follow their lead, wanting to preserve their profits by taking a temporarily precautionary approach, thus compounding the drop. For illustration purposes only, assuming the majority of stockholders held a conservative average of 60% stocks/40% bonds, if retiring investors encouraged the rest of the investors to be cautious, changing their averages to 40% stocks/60% bonds, this example could see the stock market drop over 33%!

If we take this negative view of the future, unless something is done to counter the problem, one result could be as follows:

- Millions of retirees decide to be cautious and reposition their portfolios to 20% stocks and 80% bonds.
- The stock market reacts by flattening out or potentially dropping a significant percentage.
- During a period of inflation the economy struggles.
- Individual and corporate taxes must be increased to replace lost revenue from the retirees, and pay

for Medicare and long term care needs causing the stock market to move downward.

- Investors become more cautious and move out of stocks into bonds causing the stock market to drop even more.
- In the case of all the negative ingredients occurring at once, including real estate leveling off, bonds start to struggle as companies lose capitalization, increase their liability load, and do not maintain their once high ratings. As with any free market economy, as bonds are overbought, the law of supply and demand takes over and decreases their value.
- Concerns of deflation set in.
- Federal GSE bonds (government supported enterprises such as Fannie Mae, Ginnie Mae, Freddie Mac, etc.) begin to lose value as real estate drops, and international investors sell off their huge amounts of stock and bonds.
- Though the stock market does have its upward trends, over a long period of time the economy stagnates.
- The corporations decrease in value. At this point they will need to go out and replace that loss in capital by offering more bonds. However, the greater the debt load and the lower the value of the underlying company, the fewer bond investors will be drawn to invest in those companies.
- Banks, which have experienced high growth as retirees make a dash for safety due to the federal guarantee, will begin to feel the long term negative affect as the Pension Benefit Guaranty Corporation and GSE's struggle. As some of the weaker banks falter, the FDIC begins to be drained of its guaranty funds, and Congress is

called on to once again rescue the faltering economy.

- However, in the attempt to protect the sagging national financial system, Congress will have already increased taxes and will not have much room to move without making more unpopular decisions to raise taxes. Inflation may run rampant with or without low interest rates due to the need to meet the needs of the government expenses.
- Raising taxes continues to negatively affect the economy causing multiple Recessions resulting in a Depression.

It may be one vicious spiral downward. Without major changes soon, Federal Reserve Board Chairman, Alan Greenspan warns "the adjustments could be abrupt and painful."[205]

Can Anyone Help? Please?!

If economists know what the ingredients are, then what stops them from doing all in their power to control the outcome of the future? Unfortunately, as Mr. Greenspan says, it isn't that easy. Just one financial factor alone, at any time, can affect our economy in a big way:

> Our knowledge about many of the important linkages is far from complete and in all likelihood, will always remain so. Every model, no matter how detailed or how well designed... is a vastly simplified representation of the world....

> Our problem is... [the] complexity of a world economy whose underlying linkages appear to be continuously evolving.... As we noted in our mid-1999 congressional testimony, [we chose] to focus on policies "to mitigate the fallout when it occurs and hopefully, ease the transition to the next expansion."[206]

To restate what the Fed Chairman said in May 2004: the world economy is changing and evolving so quickly it has become too difficult to get a fix on its ultimate direction. Although the public would like to think the Federal Reserve is able to steer the economy, the board is only able to make feeble attempts at limiting the temporary severity of inflation through the increase or decrease of interest rates. Even if we would like to envision that we have economists as both the engineer and brakeman on the economic train, ultimately they are passengers like every one else and have no substantial control over trends. In the end, all the government can do is let the financial system go on its way and be ready to pick up the pieces if the market should ever crash.

The U.S. economy can be likened to the fickle nature of a hurricane or tornado. Forecasters know its course, and over the short term, can warn about its general direction, but with its complexity and the myriad of prevailing external factors, the economy can veer off at the slightest provocation and could crash into a depression. Usually analysts spend their time crunching numbers from the past and can only announce where the economy has been, and even at that, the scrutiny can amazingly take six months or longer before economists are able to make their report on the present condition of the financial system.[207] For this reason, the government cautiously and often futilely tries to manipulate the economy, but has learned it can not control, let alone predict the outcome.

Proceed with Caution!

In his address at the annual Fed meeting in August, 2004, Mr. Greenspan gave his best answers to the impending economic problems expected to be caused by the aging Baby Boomers:

First, Americans must save as much as possible for a time of need. Within the lifespan of a majority of the Baby Boomers the government will not be in the position to provide the same level of pension and health care benefits as it did in the past.

Second, workers should plan on staying employed well past the age of 65 or 67. The longer retirement is delayed the better it will be for the economy.

Lastly, the Fed Chairman recommends immigration laws must be changed. He did not address the reason, but the obvious explanation is to allow more young people into the country to care for and replace the retiring elderly in the labor market.

This may be a tremendous test of collective willpower because it will mean a major shift in expectations and attitudes. However, Mr. Greenspan's proposal creates even more questions.

Can a lifetime of spending habits be changed in such a short period of time?

America has become a society of consumers, accustomed to plenty, unacquainted with frugality. Record household credit card debt confirms either a lack of control or an impractical expectation of future earnings, especially in the face of a potential economic downturn.

Will worn-out workers put off retirement for the benefit of the national economy?

Cynicism will abound if Congress passes a law to extend the retirement age significantly past 67. The Ernst & Young report, which estimates 46 million employees will take out early retirement by the year 2013, states: "This population reasonably expects to have a long and active retirement, and one quite different from that of their parents. They do not expect to scale-back their lifestyles any time soon. They are keenly interested in reinventing their lifestyles with more travel and new avocations."[208] As stated, which politician in their right mind is going to be the first to tell the retirees, "You can not retire until we tell you it is okay!"? If word gets out, this may be like shouting fire in a crowded theater. It may be a stampede of retirees as everyone rushes to the exit doors at once.
How will America respond if one out of five, twenty percent of the population, are foreign born?

Although America has had outstretched arms in the past, increasing the immigration load more than four times current levels (four to five million immigrants per year) may overload the welfare system. Although many will assimilate into society and be a benefit to the economy the average immigrant has less than a ninth-grade education[209] which may equate into millions of low-paid long term care employees who are in need of state and federal support.

Whether retirees-to-be get their way or not, the federal government might make some unpopular decisions by raising taxes, reducing benefits, and increasing immigration to preserve the future stability of America's economy. From his August meeting, Mr. Greenspan warned:

> As a nation, we owe it to our retirees to promise only the benefits that can be delivered. If we have promised more than our economy has the ability to deliver to retirees without unduly diminishing real income gains of workers, as I fear we may have, we must recalibrate our public programs so that pending retirees have time to adjust through other channels. If we delay, the adjustments could be abrupt and painful. Because curbing benefits once bestowed has proved so difficult in the past, fiscal policymakers must be especially vigilant to create new benefits only when their sustainability under the most adverse projections is virtually ensured....
>
> Responding to the pending dramatic rise in dependency ratios will be exceptionally challenging for the policymakers in developed countries. While I do not underestimate the difficulties that we face in the United States, I believe that, given

> the political will, we are better positioned than most others to make the necessary adjustments.
>
> Aside from the comparatively lesser depth of required adjustment, our open labor markets should respond more easily to the changing needs and abilities of our population; our capital markets should allow for the creation and rapid adoption of new labor-saving technologies, and our open society should be receptive to immigrants. These supports should help us adjust to the inexorabilities of an aging population. Nonetheless, tough policy choices lie ahead.[210]

Occasionally, with "cautious optimism," analysts forecast a positive trend, anticipating a robust return to the 1990s economy. "Regrettably, history is strewn with visions of such 'new eras' that, in the end, have proven to be a mirage," Greenspan noted in 1997. "In short, history counsels caution."[211]

11:59

Tick, Tick, Tick....
The Last Chapter

So, what are YOU going to do?

The ingredients for the perfect financial storm are in place. Although I hope they never come together all at once, economists are concerned about America's future as they struggle to come up with answers to the problems facing us:

- 77 million people will retiree in 18 years, of which 46 million may take early retirement by 2013. Nearly 25 million Baby Boomers have less than $1,000 of savings.
- A larger number of elderly will require more expensive health care and long term care than ever before.
- There is not enough money and too few caretakers to provide assistance to these needy Baby Boomers.
- With looming bankruptcies, Government Agencies may not be able to deliver on their promises.

- The stock market and real estate cycles are peaking and, as economists predict, are poised to flatten or go down starting around the year 2010.
- Many other negative ingredients could hasten and compound the problem such as consumer, corporate, and government debt, terrorism, global warming, and the growing energy crisis.
- Recession, stagnation, or even hyperinflation, may occur.
- Multiple recessions would lead to a depression.

What will happen to you in the worst case scenario?
What will your retirement be like?
Will your finances be protected?
Will you be prepared?

There are a lot of questions and few answers. If some government leader is able to present a viable solution that the nation will accept, then the economic problems may be diverted. However, if this storm does hit your home and you follow my simple advice to get ready, you may be inconvenienced, but your life should not be devastated.

Reviewing the facts presented in the preceding chapters I urge my friends to:

⇒ FIRST, START SAVING LIKE TOMORROW DEPENDS ON IT!

⇒ SECOND, DIVERSIFY YOUR INVESTMENTS, AND WHEN THE TIME IS RIGHT, CONSIDER ***GUARANTEED*** ACCOUNTS.

Then, if everything falls apart, at least you know you have tried to prepare.

Tomorrow's Economy

Remember these valuable points about the approaching financial storm:

- Ominous warning signs on the horizon do not mean the storm can not be diverted or, for that matter, evaporate.
- Although the storm may be slow moving and last for years, there will be sunny times again.
- Because no one knows how long the storm may last, you must prepare by saving all you can and diversifying in case any one financial source fails.
- If there is no storm, then you will have all the more resources to enjoy the future.

Like trying to forecast next week's weather, predicting the direction of our economy with any certainty is almost impossible. Even though market analysts are able to identify patterns of expansion and contraction, economic regularity is not as constant as nature's four seasons.

While economic cycles have been tracked for hundreds of years, there is no financial equinox to guide investors to determine when to plant and when to reap the harvest. The period of time between recessions varies enough to encourage investors to ride out the storm between the troughs. For example, since the 1930s there have been 13 recessions, with the average cycle between the troughs at five years, the shortest being 18 months (1981) and the longest coming in at 128 months (the 1990s). With all these cycles during this period of time, the market performed remarkably well as the Dow Jones Industrial Average increased more than 20,000% from 50 in 1932 to over 10,000 at the turn of the millennium.

Talk to anyone who lived through the Great Depression and they will undoubtedly remember how their family or friends struggled throughout the 1930s. The combination of the stock market crash, high unemployment, a major drought, and failed banks made life miserable.

The early 30s labor market may have been a disaster, but once the nation got over the shock of the bank and corporate failures, and the stock market returned to the steady growth pattern it established in the early 1920s, the previous trend resumed its course for the next four years, at least until the next recession when the impending war in Europe began to impact the market in 1937.

Although the cause of the 1930s crash is vastly different from most other recessions, analysts find valuable information in the activity of the Dow Jones Industrial Average before and after the Great Depression. Compare the 1920 to 1937 Dow Jones average chart with the NASDAQ index during a similar time frame before and after its rise and fall in 2000.

In 1920 America was just recovering from World War I. In 1990, the country was preparing for the short lived Gulf War. After both wars the economy was stirred into a buying frenzy. The automobile craze of the 20s and the Tech Boom of the 90s triggered the market to shoot up, hit a peak, and then take a freefall back to a more realistic pace. The percentage amounts are not identical, but notice the similarities in the trends of the following graphs and charts.[212]

Except for a couple of huge growth years in the technology laden NASDAQ index, its parallels with the Dow Jones Industrial Average are striking.

Dow Jones Industrial Average (1920-1937)

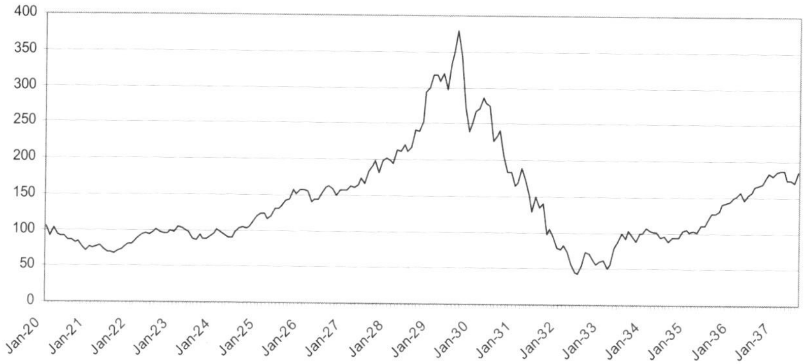

NASDAQ (1990-2007)

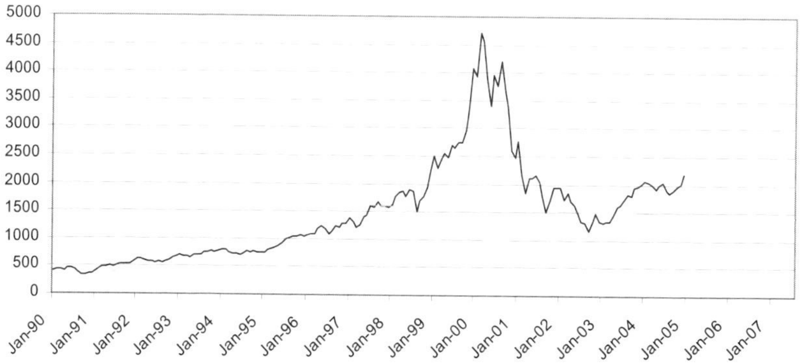

INDEX PAST PERFORMANCE IS NOT INDICATIVE OF FUTURE RESULTS.

The Rise and Fall of the 1920s Dow Jones Index And the 1990s NASDAQ

Year	Dow Jones Return	Year	NASDAQ Return
1920	-32.9%	**1990**	-17.8%
1921	12.7%	**1991**	56.8%
1922	21.7%	**1992**	15.5%
1923	-3.3%	**1993**	14.7%
1924	26.2%	**1994**	- 3.2%
1925	30.0%	**1995**	39.9%
1926	0.3%	**1996**	22.7%
1927	28.8%	**1997**	21.6%
1928	48.2%	**1998**	39.6%
1929	-17.2%	**1999**	85.6%
1930	-33.8%	**2000**	-39.3%
1931	-52.7%	**2001**	-21.1%
1932	-23.1%	**2002**	-31.5%
1933	66.7%	**2003**	52.3%
1934	4.1%	**2004**	8.6%*
1935	38.5%	**2005**	**?**
1936	24.8%	**2006**	**?**

*As of 12/30/2004

INDEX PAST PERFORMANCE IS NOT INDICATIVE OF FUTURE RESULTS.

Following the first recession of the new millennium, Alan Greenspan predicts the U.S. economy is poised for a rebound to last for a few years. However, risks remain as the country continues to be "buffeted by strong cross currents". He is "cautiously optimistic" about the short term.[213] But if hard decisions are not made soon, we will face "abrupt and painful" adjustments.[214]

Speaking to the FDIC, Dick Berner, the Chief U.S. Economist at Morgan Stanley says the economy will see "a long, slow recovery.... Much of the wealth... has dissipated." In 2003, "one-third of the world's economies [were] actually in deflation.... The FDIC needs to watch for adequate capitalization at all institutions.... There is one problem that could come out of the stock market decline that may not show up until much later – under-funded pensions. These will have to be funded before the retirement crunch comes."[215]

The National Center for Policy Analysis looks past the short term upswing and once again negatively declares, "As the payroll tax spirals, the economic opportunity of children and grandchildren will be pitted against the financial security of their parents and grandparents and everyone will lose."[216]

Are You Ready For The Retirement Rush?

Economists are doubtful the stock market will repeat the frantic growth of the 1990s until the world invents another economic powerhouse. In the late 1920s the automobile industry helped drive the stock market up before it finally crashed. In the 90s the computer and internet industries electrified the market. Until the perfection of some alternative fuel, medical advancement, or other innovation that everyone wants, the economy will probably slump into a slower pace.

Dr. Robert Goodman is known for his often accurate forecast of the future. In 1980, he agreed with Sir John Templeton that the stock market (the Dow Jones Industrial Average) would move from its stagnant level at 800 points and double four times in the next 20 years to reach 10,000! Sure enough, it happened.[217]

In 2001, Dr. Goodman predicted the market could double again, maybe. However, this time he warns the growth may be hindered by taxes and will be followed by the possibility of a worldwide Depression brought on by a cascade of events which could be well on their way by the year 2012. These events could actually start three or four years before as the world anticipates the date.

Will it happen? Who knows? But the prudent will at least prepare. The warning voice has been sounded for years. The concern of many economists and analysts is that this depression could last for more than a decade. The turbulence could begin as early as 2008 or sooner, with the rough ride possibly lasting from 2010 to 2022. Doctors Goodman, Shiller, Campbell, and others predict a number of successive recessions during this period which could make the Great Depression of the 1930s seem mild in comparison.[218]

This potential financial downturn does not even take into consideration skyrocketing federal and state debt, as well as a bankrupt Medicare and Social Security system. Coupled with this dismal financial future, Americans have not tried hard enough to save for retirement. There is concern that Baby Boomers are borrowing more and saving less than ever before. The average household credit card balance is so huge that it could take up to two decades to pay off at current levels.[219]

Even though the financial time bomb continues ticking, as long as you know where to go for protection there is no reason to fear the eventual outcome. Americans are too resilient to allow such a challenge to get in the way of their long term happiness. Yet this does not mean tomorrow's test will not be a trial!

There is at least a ray of hope, one positive trend that most economists are looking forward to in the short term. As the upcoming retirees finally realize the importance of saving for their future, they will begin to save and invest like never before, which will drive up the market in the years preceding the retirement rush.

So, this is my challenge to you:

- Make the commitment that your savings will never be squandered for temporary amusement at the risk of your future comfort and lifestyle. Unless needed for your essential living expenses, be cautious to never spend money you may need tomorrow.
- Learn to control your spending habits.
- Start today. Do not wait any longer.

If you have not been saving, it is not too late, as long as you begin ***now***.

Start Saving For Your Trip

Often I hear clients say, "I need to save money for retirement," or, "I need more money so I can enjoy my retirement."

Not sure what their goals are I ask, "What do you want to do, where do you want to go, and how much money do you want to spend?"

"Oh, I don't know," is the uncertain reply, "About what I am living on now."

This type of conversation is much like a wanna-be-tourist going to a travel agent and saying, "Send me someplace nice and fun. And no, I don't know where I want to go or what I want to do."

For this reason, investment advisors end up being a lot like travel agents. Good agents and advisors will try to communicate rather than dictate. They will ask what you like and probe into your preferences and budget.

Here is a simple approach I use to help my clients identify the right destination and the most appropriate vehicle to get there. As a disclaimer, these examples are not perfect, and there are many variables that enter into the picture, but I think you will get the idea.

First, to advise you about your retirement, I need to know where you want to go and how soon you want to leave. Second, how fast do you want to get there? And then, once you arrive, what do you want to do and how long do you want to stay there?

For example, it is important for me to know whether you want to travel to Alaska or Hawaii. Your ultimate destination will affect your lifestyle and activities, as well as how you get there. I will need to know whether your trip is going to be a short or long vacation. (You would want your money in liquid or "non-qualified" accounts such as regular bank, annuity or brokerage accounts). If you want to go there for an extended period, say for retirement, you will treat your budget differently. (This would be frozen or "qualified" accounts like IRAs, 401(k)s, TSAs, 403(b)s, etc.).

If you want to go to Alaska, I have five general ways for you to get there. We can send you by a jumbo jet or charter airline. Both are fast, but still have drawbacks and risks. (This mode of transportation is similar to securities – individual stocks and bonds, mutual funds or variable annuities). I could recommend a cruise ship (compare to variable annuities with guaranteed riders) or a train ride (like a fixed annuity). Cruises and trains are usually safer, but they take longer and are harder to get off before the destination. (For that matter you don't want to take a walk outside of your airliner at thirty thousand feet – hence, you can see this isn't a perfect analogy, but the basic concept still makes sense.) A bus tour may take longer, and will not have the accommodations. In the long run you might spend more money because you have to stop and eat and sleep on the way, but again, you don't have to worry about some of the other risks. You put your faith in the driver and expect everything to be fine. (Associate the bus with a bank certificate of deposit). Finally, you could drive your own vehicle (relate this with savings accounts). You may have more flexibility, because you can stop anytime along the way, but there are a number of other factors to take into consideration, such as the wear and tear on your vehicle, including the extra money for meals and lodging, and other expenses.

So, after all this discussion, you still want to go to Hawaii? Well, that changes things. You have to save a little more money, and in addition, you better not be afraid of flying or ocean liners, because you can not take the train, bus, or car.

Get the picture?

No matter what your ultimate goal, when it comes to your financial future, my advice is: Save! Save! Save! And do it now! But don't make it hard. Saving can be as enjoyable as when you set aside some extra money for vacation. Consider every dime you put away today will add up to help your enjoyment in the future. Reconsider anything unnecessary. Do you really need that extra cup of coffee, can of soda, or candy bar? Within ten years, five dollars a day can add up to thousands of dollars, not to mention saving a lot of calories!

Prepare For The Worst.
Invest For The Best.

Looking back to the 1930s, many smart investors wisely positioned their money for success. Rather than losing a major portion of their portfolio by riding out the storm, they moved their money into safe havens, and prepared their assets to buy into solid investments when the market appeared to bottom out.

While millions were going broke during the Great Depression, some "lucky" investors became rich as they took advantage of Dr. Goodman's formula:

Crisis + Change = Opportunity

> How should investors interpret crises in financial markets? History shows that crisis leads to change and change produces opportunity. By keeping these past events in mind, investors can learn to

> use the opportunities when turmoil occurs.
> In each of these crises, the media and public perception foretold doom, but each problem was ultimately resolved by unexpected government action. In the same way, world governments will do whatever it takes to remedy the current international problems.... Make no mistake, it might take a long time, and some companies will fail, but economies will not be left in ruin.[220]

Those planning on a comfortable retirement must keep sight of their long-term perspectives and invest in those organizations that will weather the storm. By identifying the right companies, advisors say, investors can come out ahead in the end.

That is easy to say, if you are aware of your choices.

Your Options: Do It Yourself or Get Help

With over 8,000 stocks to choose from and nearly two times that many mutual funds and other investment alternatives, someone needs to be aware of the right choice.[221] That is the value of finding an investment advisor you can trust.

I have found that about one out of every two people reading this, will say, "If I take care of my investments myself, I will save a lot of money. End of discussion."

If you know what you are doing, saving money is a good idea. But it is not always less expensive to avoid professional advice, expecting to learn the intricacies of the financial markets by an occasional glance through a finance magazine.

Over the years I have learned there are some jobs I can easily do, and others I could do but don't want to do. I don't need to have someone fill up my vehicle with gas. However, I don't want to put on new tires. I know how, but I don't have the right equipment, time or energy. The more mature I get, the more realistic I become.

Here's a quick example: One late Saturday afternoon, a few years ago, my son Daniel, a teenager at the time, came in the house and told me his car's battery was running low. After taking it to the auto parts store, it was determined he needed a new alternator. I had changed an alternator before. I wanted to show him how he could save a lot of money by learning how to fix his own car. It was a matter of a few bolts, a new belt, maybe an hour of time, and a great way to bond with my son. We got the car home and into the garage. Proudly, I told him what was going to happen and that we would have the job done in no time -- as we began working on a car I had never worked on before.

I found the bolts holding the alternator on, and noticed that there was a big metal plate in the way. I began to loosen each bolt. I was surprised that the bolts were unusually longer than those I had seen in the past but they were coming out, so I kept on with my task. As I was about to take the last bolt off, suddenly, the whole engine block dropped with a thud.

Stunned, I took a step back, and realized I had just taken off the motor mounts, something I had never done before. I had graduated summa cum laude from both a major university and the School of Hard Knocks, but nothing in my schooling had prepared me for this one.

Wanting to bond, rather than have a meltdown, I somewhat calmly explained what I had just done to Daniel, who's only response was, "Oh-Oh!" About eight hours later, at 2:00 in the morning, I finally figured out how to lift a thousand pound engine back in place.

My lesson learned? Sometimes it is better to pay a hundred dollars to have an expert do the job and save you hours of needless work and headache.

My recommendation: If you are able, go ahead and write your own checks, balance your checkbook, and give approval of the final investment decisions. But unless you have the time and resources to research thousands of companies, I encourage you to seriously consider a professional advisor. Even if there are investments which are "no-load" and do not charge, you may want to have an advisor review your choices to make sure that you have not overlooked an investment which might be better suited for you.

And what is the success ratio of an individual trying to invest on their own?

One analysis, from a large investment firm, showed what happens when professional investment advice is not obtained and how people let their emotions get in the way, often resulting in below market average returns:

> With most investors, a constant struggle occurs between a desire to pursue short term gains at the expense of a long-term strategy....
>
> When designing your portfolio, having a short-term perspective can not only provide undue anxiety and constant attention to performance, but it can also do considerable damage to the growth potential of your investments. Many investors make the mistake of frequently adjusting their portfolio usually because they desire to chase a hot investment of the moment or because they are fleeing downturns.
>
> Short investment holding periods are the chief reason that investors under-performed the market indexes. Working with an investment representative can have the investors develop a more disciplined approach, designing a portfolio that is consistent with your goals and risk profile, giving you less reason to chase performance.[222]

Because they do not have the time to be aware of their available options, investors often worry they have not made the right choices. Without up-to-date knowledge, greed and fear encourages irrational decisions.

Over a twenty year period, investors averaged only 2.6% each year, when the S&P 500 index made 12.2% over that same period of time!

Profile of an Equity Investor (1983 to 2003)[223]

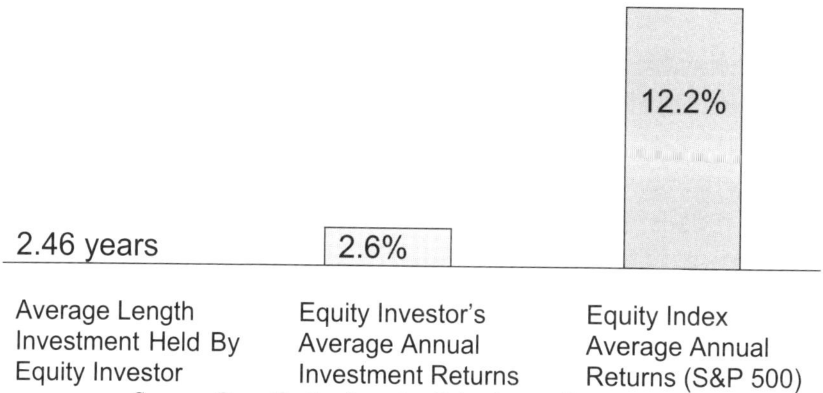

Source: Quantitative Investor Behavior, Dalbar, 2003.
INDEX PAST PERFORMANCE IS NOT INDICATIVE OF FUTURE RESULTS.

When a professional is responsible for your investments, they will normally be more patient and often, a lot more cautious. Contrary to what you might hear at the water cooler or in the media, most advisors have the perspective to understand:

> No matter what I do, there are some things
> I can not control.

In fact there are many things beyond our control. The advisor can not control, and normally won't be able to anticipate surprise decisions by the Federal Reserve, the fluctuating value of real estate, the constantly changing Internal Revenue Service codes, the closing price of your favorite stock, the uncertainty of pension plans, inflation, deflation, unemployment, and corporate and government debt. These are just a few of the financial issues neither the investor nor the financial consultant has any control over.

Still, an investment advisor is able to maintain a “clear perspective” and help you:

- Calculate your financial needs and plan your financial goals
- Determine a suitable mix of investments to achieve your goals
- Ensure that you are not taking an unnecessary amount of risk to reach your goals
- Maintain financial discipline in the face of Bull Market exuberance and Bear Market despair
- Educate you on different types of investments and their tax implications.[224]

However, before you finally choose an advisor, you should make sure he or she is empathetic, is capable of being sympathetic, and hopefully not pathetic when it comes to communication. This ability to connect is essential when it comes to expressing a goal and seeing it implemented. Normally, a degree or “certification” does not guarantee that the advisor or accountant is a communicator. That decision will be totally up to you to decide.

What Should YOU Do?

Whether you are a do-it-yourselfer or someone who knows their limitations and when to ask for help, the best advice I can give is simple: Don’t Wait! Start Saving Now! It may be the only answer for your financial security.

Alan Greenspan has presented his one and only plan for Baby Boomers to prepare for the coming retirement crisis. Mr. Greenspan recommended that Americans: 1) increase personal savings and carefully budget expenses, 2) work longer than age 65 or 67, and 3) accept more immigrants into the country to replace the retirees in the workforce. This acceptance will also provide entry level long-term caretakers for the elderly.

As the Fed Chairman encouraged Americans to seriously save for their future, he also recommended they pass their investment and retirement accounts to their beneficiaries through some long term plan.

Although he did not specifically mention Revocable Trusts or a beneficiary annuity, he did make clear that spending it all or dumping a lump sum amount of money in the lap of a beneficiary will be bad for the economy. He said, trusts and annuities will benefit the retiree, the beneficiaries, and the national economy.[225]

> A key component of domestic saving in the United States in future decades will be the path of the personal saving rate. That rate will depend on a number of factors, especially the behavior of the members of the baby-boom cohort during their retirement years.... Often people bequeath a significant proportion of their savings to their children or others rather than spend it during retirement. If the baby-boom generation continues this pattern, achieving a higher private domestic saving rate is not out of reach.[226]

Many insurance companies offer what is often called the "Legacy" benefit of a fixed or variable annuity.

This feature provides a way for the retiring owner to use the money during their life, and if there is any money left over, to pass along the remaining assets to the spouse, then on to successive beneficiaries knowing they will receive monthly payments until it is depleted. In addition, death benefits and other optional lifetime guarantees will provide an important safety net to the family.

How Do You Prepare?

When preparing for the uncertain time ahead, look for investments which are guaranteed and liquid. A "guarantee" on your money normally means you are going to have to pay a premium, but remember, you pay for what you get. The more liquid your account – in other words, the easier chance you have of getting to your money (your assets are not frozen) – the more risk you usually have to accept if you want to make more money. An aggressive investment style is not appropriate for all investors. It would be helpful to speak an investment advisor to identify your risk tolerance.

Invest and Save Take advantage of the short term economic growth which may occur before the Baby Boomers retire. Be aggressive in your investment style over the short term and you may see impressive results. There may be a few downtrends, but according to Ned Davis, Harry Dent, and others, the expected pattern is positive leading up to 2009 to 2010. Decennial Trends, a potential new energy saving economy and good old greed may drive the market.

As the second decade draws closer each investor must be prepared to either have their investments in guaranteed accounts or be ready to move in and out of the market with dexterity. To be a smart investor you will have to watch out for your own nest egg. To protect yourself you'll need to get out of the market at the best time. No one knows when that will be. There may be a number of sucker rallies during this time which will play on both the greed and fear of all investors increasing the volatility of the market.

This style of investing will require constant vigilance on your part. Still, it is never wise to expect someone else to watch out for your investments. A smart investor will obtain professional investment advice from someone who can watch your investment as if it was their own.

One client told me, “I read and read and read about stocks, and it seems like there is just so much to learn.”

My response was, “Don’t feel bad if you never learn it all, because it is a myth to believe someone is a market expert. The stock market is pure emotion. There is no way to get a handle on it or get your arms around it. The market is not a rational entity that you can understand.” Sure, we can watch patterns, but you never know which way a skittish or stampeding herd is going to go.

He wisely responded, “I guess you have to detach yourself from it. You just can’t get yourself too involved.”

Know When To Sell Once you commit to memory that the up and down movement of the stock market is natural it will be much easier to be emotionally prepared when the economy starts to head down. That doesn't mean you should sit and do nothing. It is okay to sell when your security reaches a predetermined level. Just don't panic.

Many investment advisors feel there is nothing you can do about a downturn in the stock market. Normally these "buy and hold" advisors remind their clients that the market will eventually come back. Still, "understanding how common shifts in the market have been is important for realistic expectations."[227]

The following chart reminds us that if you are going to be invested in the stock market, expect a five percent or more drop more than three times a year, and at least a ten percent drop once per year. Big drops in the market happen every two or three years. Still, the market has moved forward.

Bull Markets vs. Bear Markets
2/20/1928 - 5/24/2004

	Bull	Bear
Avg. Length (Years)	2.5	0.7
Avg. Return (Cum. Return %)	154%	-33%

	Occurrences	Num./Yr.
Bull Market (Gain of 20%+)	24	0.3
Dip (Decline of 5%+)	256	3.4
Correction (Decline of 10%+)	87	1.1
Severe Correction (15%+ Decline)	38	0.5
Bear Market (20%+ Decline)	23	0.3

INDEX PAST PERFORMANCE IS NOT INDICATIVE OF FUTURE RESULTS. Assumes reinvestment of capital gains and dividends and no taxes. The Index is unmanaged and unavailable for direct investment. Data source: Ned Davis Research, 6/04

This is precisely why you need to spread your money out if you expect to use your investment any time soon, or if you want it protected.

Diversify Prepare for any potential economic downturn by diversifying your assets with the help of your investment advisor. Never have more than a third of your portfolio invested in real estate or other illiquid assets. Spread your portfolio throughout Short, Mid and Long-Term Investments.

Own your own home, but do not overdo Real Estate as it is just as risky and uncertain as other investments. I regularly have clients say, "But my real estate has never gone down! I made thousands of dollars in a short period of time!" Do not forget the 1980s when the Federal Savings and Loan institutions collapsed leaving vast tracts of homes empty as their value plummeted.

Another example from the 1980s was California's Prop 13, a tax referendum, which resulted in the devaluation of real estate for millions of property owners. In some cases real estate dropped over 50% in value. When large amounts of money are tied up in real estate it can literally take years before a sale occurs to provide the needed cash.

Many investors get confused when it comes to knowing where to put their funds. First, remember, when you work with an investment advisor, they will often be able to diversify your portfolio. Too many investors incorrectly believe they need more than one investment advisor to be cautious. The bottom line is your advisor should be spreading your investment across a number of different companies. Just as you wouldn't want more than one cook in the kitchen (who decides how much salt or spices is "enough"?) you also don't want conflicting efforts from multiple advisors.

Then, don't become confused by the investment options that are available. With all the advertising that goes on, remember that it really is not that difficult. There are three industries where you can place your cash investments, all watched over by state and federal agencies: the Banking Industry, the Insurance Industry, and the Securities Industry, which monitors the stock and bond market.

Where Do You Invest?

Here is a simple way to remember what each investment will do for you. The interest rates quoted are a general guesstimate only and may vary:

Banks The majority of America has their money safely kept in **Savings and Checking Accounts** at nearly 10,000 banks across the country. The obvious reason most people are satisfied with keeping their money with a bank or thrift institution is because they are guaranteed by the FDIC, the Federal Deposit Insurance Corporation. Although the FDIC may experience financial problems during a depression, the banking industry should still be supported by the taxpayer, just as in the past. Just don't put all your eggs in one basket, which includes banks.

Because banks provide expensive services and invest in long term bonds and real estate mortgages, the rate of return on savings accounts is lower. In "average" years, the rate of **Certificate of Deposits** will normally fluctuate from 3% to 5%, occasionally bumping up past 6% when inflation gets too high. The rates may be higher or lower depending on the length of time you leave the money in the CD.

Insurance Annuities, often referred to as "pension" or "retirement" accounts, are the investment instruments offered by insurance companies. They may be fixed or variable annuities, guaranteed by the insurance company, and backed by re-insurers, insurance companies which promise to be a safety net if the primary company struggles and is unable to make payment. Annuities are not as liquid and may be subject to a 10% IRS penalty if money is withdrawn before age 59½. You need to be careful with annuities, because some companies will not allow withdrawals without long-term annuitization.

Fixed Annuities come in a few versions, but are best described as similar to a bank CD, however, they are not guaranteed by the FDIC. The interest rates are usually one or more percentage points higher than what the bank will pay, averaging around 4% to 6% or more. Fixed annuities have terms of five to fifteen years, so they require longer commitment. Ten percent withdrawals are normally available each year without a surrender charge, which provide more flexibility than a CD.

Variable Annuities are a combination of insurance and securities, where your premium dollar purchases a part of an investment account, which in some cases is very similar to the mutual funds they are patterned after. A Variable Annuity is an "umbrella account" which holds multiple sub-accounts, with investment options ranging from Cash to Bonds and Stock accounts. Just like Fixed Annuities, a VA allows withdrawals with no surrender charge. Most companies have ready access accounts which allow you to withdraw at no charge, as long as you are over the 59½ age bracket.

The best value of a Variable Annuity is the death benefit and the new living benefit guarantees. When someone dies, holding an account with a death benefit, the insurance company guarantees that the client will get their deposit back, and sometimes they would even get a minimum interest rate, even if the stock sub-accounts ended up lower than the original investment (less withdrawals and expenses). For a fee of about ½%, the living benefit guarantee offers the client a safety net. If the account goes down, they are guaranteed their original deposit. If it goes up they receive the higher amount. In many cases there is even a step up where the account locks in occasional profits at a new guaranteed level. The guarantee varies by company but is an excellent option to consider.

Because you pay for what you get, the ready access and guarantees often mean higher hidden fees. Researchers show the benefits of a variable annuity costs about 8/10 of one percent more than the average mutual fund. Some people prefer to think of this as the cost of insurance to make sure their money is guaranteed.

Studies also frequently show annuities are less expensive as they are tax deferred entities and over time save on taxes. [228] Variable Annuities are not FDIC insured and the guarantee is based on the claims-paying ability of the issuing insurance company. This is why it is important to review the strength and rating of each company.

Just as a bank's Certificate of Deposit has penalties for early withdrawal, most annuities have surrender charges. Ask your investment advisor to identify the Variable Annuities which provide immediate access without a charge. Finally, remember that annuities are designed to be retirement products. If you withdraw your money before age 59½ the IRS may levy a 10% penalty.

Securities Industry While stock and bond investments are not guaranteed, they do have the most potential for growth because, other than sales and purchase charges, they do not have extra "benefits" attached. There are a number of ways you can buy a stock or bond. You can purchase the securities directly from the company or organization. You may buy stocks or bonds through an investment advisor which uses a large exchange (such as the New York Stock Exchange, or NASDAQ), or you may have an investment manager combine them with a group of other stocks through a mutual fund. See Appendix 4 for a brief review of the costs of owning securities.

Stocks, or "equities," provide the most potential for growth. Looking at the historical chart, even with all their wild ups and downs, stocks over a 50 year period have nearly doubled bonds.

Here is a brief primer on securities. When you purchase a stock, you own a portion or "share" of a company. Of course, depending on how well the company does in any one quarter or year, you have a greater potential for making money, but if the company does poorly, you can also lose your investment if you sell out at the wrong time.

Bonds, on the other hand, have normally been safer offering less volatility. A bond is nothing more than a loan to an organization where you are promised a regular payment for your loan. Bonds can be purchased from Corporate or Government Entities. For example, there are Corporate Bonds, Municipal Bonds, Treasury Bills and Bonds, and Government Sponsored Entities Bonds such as GinnieMae, FannieMae, and FreddieMac.

Bonds are the safer investment over time because if a company takes out bankruptcy, federal rules and regulations require the company to sell off its assets and with any money left over, pay creditors first.

A **Mutual Fund**, in its simplest form, is an account held by an investment company that manages a group of either stocks, bonds, or a combination of both. While there are over 8,000 stocks listed through the various exchanges, depending on the year, there are 15-20,000 or more mutual funds. The Mutual Fund is a private company which invests your money in multiple securities for a fee. Appendix 4 goes into detail about the different types of mutual funds and their costs.

Most serious investors prefer to trade individual securities, while smaller accounts, such as a lone IRA account, are more cost effective if diversified through a mutual fund.

Investment Style

As you prepare for your future, remember to be patient. Whether your money is in a savings account, an insurance annuity, stocks or bonds, real estate, or any number of other vehicles, your investment success is dependent on your clear goal and consistent plan. While there are volumes written about "buy and hold" and "active trading" methods, a successful portfolio is dependent on the attention you give it. Each method has its place. But once you put your money to work, wherever you decide, if you ignore it, you may not end up where you would like.

The bottom line is to avoid fear and greed and to not search for unrealistic results. One CNBC commentator advised, "There are no truths, only risks. Three down years don't guarantee an up year. Buy-and-hold forever is no guarantee of success. And interest-rate cuts guarantee nothing... absolutely nothing."[229]

Where Should You Invest Your Money?

So many choices and so many confusing voices!

The following bar chart is similar to those found in many mutual fund or variable annuity sales brochures. Its purpose is to encourage you to see the long term benefit of keeping your funds invested in stocks or equities. Many investors are wary of the sales pitch, because they have been through the volatile ride and worry they could actually lose money if they take their money out at the wrong time.

The line graph on the next page, although it is a generalized illustration, gives a better view of what may happen. Placing your money in an FDIC guaranteed bank certificate of deposit will result in a lower return represented by Treasury Bonds "Cash Investment" which normally returns a slightly better interest rate. A fixed annuity, guaranteed and re-insured by insurance companies, will usually make more, with no fluctuation if left to maturity.

Keep in mind, though, banks and insurance companies have only a limited number of places they can invest their money, namely, real estate mortgage loans and bonds, business loans, and occasionally some blue chip stocks.

While bonds may be more consistent, they can still fluctuate, even if they are offered by the federal or state governments. Bonds can lose 5% or more in any given year. Finally, stocks have always outperformed all the other options by almost double the return. But with equities vacillating up and down by more than 20%, they are not a good investment for the short term, if you need to use the money any time soon.

While the following chart makes it appear that your best place to invest is stocks, it is important to remember that the investment value will fluctuate over time. This is why stocks or "equities" are a long term investment. Since 1789 the stock market has demonstrated there is a very good chance that your stock portfolio will eventually go up. But a purchase today could be at its high point. The stocks or bonds in your account could drop causing your investment balance to go down for months or years.

Average Annual Returns (12/31/53–12/31/03)

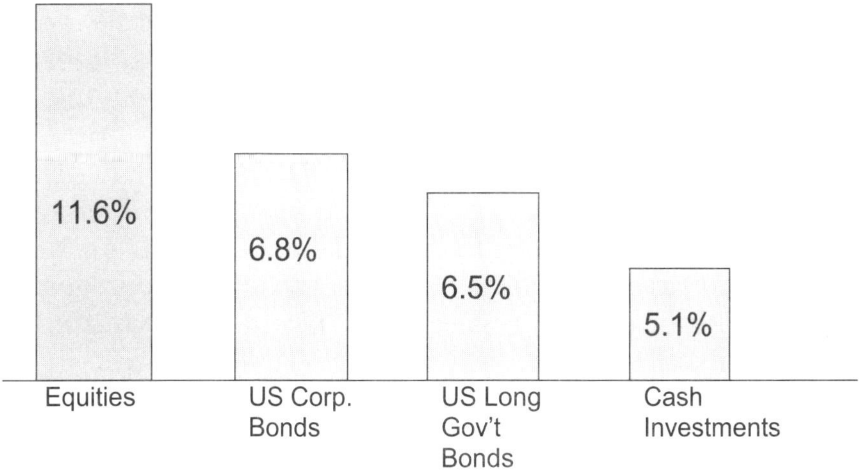

INDEX PAST PERFORMANCE IS NOT INDICATIVE OF FUTURE RESULTS. Investment value will fluctuate so that shares, when redeemed, may be worth more or less their original cost. The above indices are unmanaged and unavailable for direct investment. Data source: Wiesenberger, 6/04. Not to scale.

This is why you must sit down with your investment advisor and identify what types of risk you are able to handle.

Either Way, Investing or Saving Is Risky!

There are a number of risks which can affect your long term investment goals:

- **Volatility Risk**: This is the up and down price value of an investment. You may purchase it at one price, and within moments, it may make or lose money. The expectation is that over time the position will move in an upward trend, but it is any persons guess when that may happen. Real Estate and Securities may lose value in the short-term.

- **Tax Risk**: Each year the Internal Revenue Service will ask you to pay taxes on the ordinary and capital gains in your account. While you thought you made a lot of money on the sale of a stock or mutual fund, you may end up paying a sizeable amount of taxes on your profit. Although you may think you can use a capital loss against your income, your advisor may show how the loss may be limited because you do not have enough gains in the same tax category. Make sure you review your plans with your tax advisor before you make a sudden decision.
- **Inflation Risk**: Earning two percent in a "safe" account, during a period of time when the Consumer Price Index shows three percent inflation, would actually result in a loss of buying power. During the 50 year period of December 31, 1953 to December 31,2003 inflation averaged 3.92%. Making a "safe" 2% in a savings or money market could actually lose almost 2% in your account! The same thing happens if you lock your money in a vault. That's not very safe! [230]
- **Longevity Risk**: The period of time an account is held is looked at in two ways: charges or losses you may incur if you try to cash in the investment too soon, or an agreement made to which locks the funds up for a certain period of time. Real Estate may seem to be "safe", but depending on the market, may not sell for months or years. An account may also be at risk from a combination of the other risks. Investment firms warn "the greatest risk is actually produced by taxes and inflation together – the risk of not having enough money to last through retirement."[231]

So, where do you invest? The bottom line is based on when you need to use your money. Here are some points to consider:

Banks

Offer Certificates of Deposits, Savings Accounts, and Money Markets
Advantages: Insured by the FDIC
Disadvantages: Inflation Risk, Tax Risk, and Longevity Risk.
Higher rates require longer terms
The interest paid by banks may drop at renewal depending on the economy

Annuities – Variable and Fixed

Advantages: Not insured by the FDIC, but guaranteed by the claims-paying ability of the insurance company.
Fixed Annuities pay more than CDs
Disadvantages: Inflation Risk on Variable Annuities, Longevity Risk on Fixed Annuities.
Higher rates, require longer terms

Bonds

Advantages: Steady Interest Earnings
Disadvantages: Not guaranteed, Lower rates of return than equities, Volatility Risk

Stocks

Advantages: Highest Return
Disadvantages: Greatest Volatility Risk, Long term investment, Tax Risk

A well-planned investment can satisfy both your goals and risk tolerance. Each of these investment categories will have different results over the short and long term, each affected by the different types of risk.

Income or Loss Comparison Between Stocks and Bonds (Mutual Funds and Variable Annuities), Fixed Annuities, and CD's

For Illustration Purposes Only

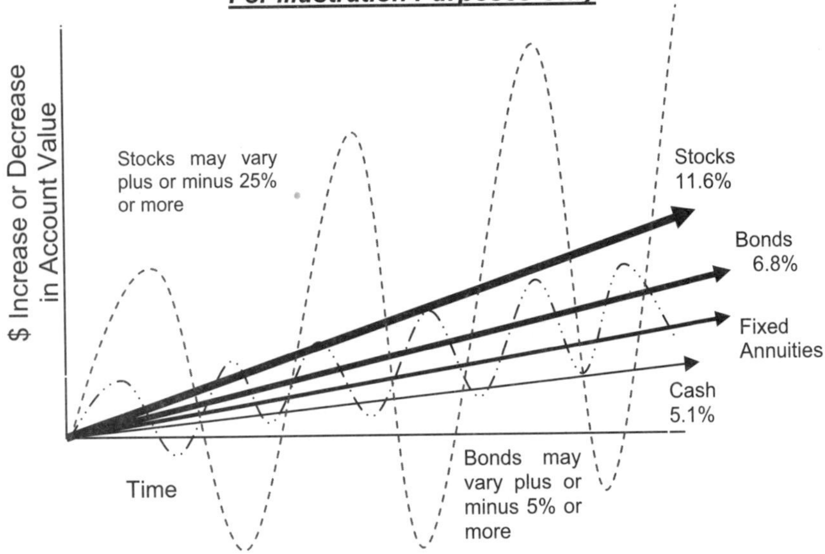

Each of the asset classes have different risk-return profiles as well other characteristics, such as high liquidity (cash investments), regular fixed payments (bonds), and company ownership (equities). Your investment representative can help you understand the differences and suitability for each type.

[3]Equities represented by the S&P 500 Index. [4]U.S. Corporate Bonds represented by Salomon Brothers Corporate Bonds Index, which is a Salomon index of long-term corporate, high grade industrial and utility bonds rated Aa or better with an average maturity of approximately 23 years. [5]U.S. Long-term Government Bonds represented by Lehman Brothers Long Government Index, which is based upon all publicly issued long-term government debt securities. [6]Cash investments are represented by 90-Day U.S. Treasury Bills. Assumes reinvestment of capital gains and dividends and no taxes. Money market funds are not insured or guaranteed by the Federal Deposit Insurance Corporation (FDIC) or any other government agency. Although the funds seek to preserve the value of the investment at $1.00 per share, it is possible to lose money by investing in the funds. INDEX PAST PERFORMANCE IS NOT INDICATIVE OF FUTURE RESULTS. Investment value will fluctuate so that shares, when redeemed, may be worth more or less their original cost. The above indices are unmanaged and unavailable for direct investment. Data source: Wiesenberger, 6/04.

As you can see, you can make more money with stocks and bonds, but you can also lose money if you sell at the wrong time. If you tend to worry, do not invest in securities that are not guaranteed. Spending an hour with an investment advisor, identifying your changing lifestyle and needs, as well as your "risk tolerance," will be valuable to your future peace of mind.

Look for Protection!

How do you prepare for an uncertain future? The answer is to diversify your portfolio into accounts which are backed by strong assets or companies which will not be worthless if the perfect storm strikes. You may not be in the position to do this today, but with planning, you may be able to prepare for tomorrow.

This is the Warning Voice:

- Watch for signs of a major economic downturn.
- Until that time, take advantage of any growth in the economy.
- Be as aggressive as you can with stocks and mutual funds.
- Keep your portfolio diversified. Do not over extend yourself in any one area.
- Invest in guaranteed accounts before the guarantees are discontinued.
- Pay off your home mortgage with a lump sum payment when you can.
- Live prudently.

There is nothing shrill or harsh about this message. I am not telling you to run faster than you are able. My advice is to watch out for the uncertainty of the future, make a plan and stick to it. This is nothing more than the wise counsel our ancestors understood: Save in a time of plenty; prepare for a time of famine. Again, diversification is the answer. Diversity does not mean you need to use different financial advisors. When your consultant spreads your portfolio over a variety of investments you are being cautious.

Consider dividing your assets between insured investments and real estate, both held for the long term. Use checking and savings accounts primarily for short-term living expenses. Protect your retirement by using annuities and mutual funds guaranteed by the claims paying ability of quality insurance companies.

Here are some final points:

Real Estate

- Own your home without a mortgage. Put aside extra money in an investment account to pay off your house as soon as you can. Don't be persuaded to make a bi-weekly mortgage payment. Banks usually make more money than you in this plan. (See Appendix 3) Remember, early principal payments normally do not earn interest. It is better to deposit your money in a savings or investment account where it may grow and stay ahead of inflation.
- Do not use up your entire portfolio to pay off your home. Keep at least six months of your budget readily available. You can't eat wood and bricks.
- Consider investing in a rental property or in REITs, Real Estate Investment Trusts purchased from an investment advisor. Be careful you do not get sold into thinking this is the only way to invest your money. There are risks involved. Once you own real estate it can take months to years to get your money out of it. In addition, how will you pay the mortgage if the economy struggles, your renters lose work, and you are not able to find someone to make the payments? Think what will happen to your credit when you are under this kind of financial pressure.

- If interest rates go up or the economy crashes into a depression, do not be caught with a mortgage that you are unable to pay. Remember the 1930s and the 1980s; in many cases people couldn't give their real estate away.

Bank Accounts

- The safety of an insured money market account or certificate of deposit means nothing when your account does not keep up with inflation. Do not lock your money into long-term, low paying CDs. Consider laddering your CDs over a number of years.
- Spread out your savings into strong banks which will not be hindered by troubles caused by poorly managed corporate holdings, such as a failing mortgage or credit card division.
- Be careful your accounts do not exceed the maximum insured protection.
- Banks, thrifts and credit unions do fail. Over the short-term, the FDIC will protect your bank account up to the limit allowed by law. But a guarantee does not mean the bank will never go bankrupt. Make sure you diversify your money into other guaranteed investments to protect your assets during a long recession.
- High rates do not equate with well managed banks or safe investments. Sometimes new and expanding companies will offer risky high rates to get your business. Be careful of the FDIC's "moral hazard". Investment Advisors offer FDIC insured Brokered CDs, often with highly rated companies at rates above what is available from local banks. These CDs can lose money if cashed out before maturity.

Insured Accounts

- Insured accounts normally earn more than what you would receive from a bank account, but they are not insured by a Government Subsidized Entity, such as the FDIC.
- A well-diversified insured portfolio will include fixed and variable annuities or mutual funds which are monitored by state and federal agencies, and guaranteed by a well managed, highly rated insurance company.
- Fixed and variable annuities are designed for retirement after age 59½. While they are tax deferred like an IRA, they may also have surrender or withdrawal charges if your annuity is not an accessible account. Not all annuities require long term commitments. Before retirement, the IRS will levy a 10% penalty in addition to taxes if withdrawn too soon.
- Work only with advisors who are licensed to offer both fixed and variable annuities. If the advisor has your interests in mind they will present the best options available.
- Invest in the stock and bond market through Variable Annuities. Think about paying a little extra for an insurance policy to guarantee your initial deposit during your lifetime. The cost of this living benefit is about ½%. The best variable annuity insurance companies offer a safety net on stock and bond investment accounts for a fee. These guarantees, like most special offers, may not always be available, so it is important that you open an account that permits additional guaranteed investments before they are discontinued.

- Occasionally mutual fund companies will present managed funds which are guaranteed by an insurance company. They are excellent for those people who are concerned about the future and want to have their money liquid enough to get to it. These funds provide protection of principal and investment gains at maturity. In spite of the guarantee there are circumstances under which such a fund could lose principal especially if you invest in the fund then withdraw your money before the due date. If taken out too soon, a shareholder could receive upon redemption the future Net Asset Value (NAV) which may be lower than the value at maturity or lower than the initial investment. The financial condition of the guaranteeing insurance company is critical in your evaluation and regular monitoring of such a product. Carefully read the prospectus of any fund before purchasing it. Not all funds are created equal, and some may be better than others.

As long as you are being cautious remember to pay your own way and keep some extra money on hand for a rainy day. Former Secretary of Agriculture, Ezra T. Benson, an expert on prudent living, who assisted the starving Europeans after World War II, encouraged Americans to avoid speculation, save up money and have enough food and clothing on hand just in case they were hit by unemployment or there was a run on grocery stores and prices skyrocketed. He warned:

> History has demonstrated that in difficult days it is reserves with intrinsic value that are of most worth, rather than reserves, the value of which may be destroyed

> through inflation. It is well to remember that continued government deficits cause inflation; inflation is used as an excuse for ineffective price controls; price controls lead to shortages; artificial shortages inevitably are used as an excuse to implement rationing.[232]

I have learned the cost of a can of baked beans can increase more than 10% in a year. That is a return that even the best of investors could appreciate.

IF YOU ARE PREPARED YOU SHALL NOT FEAR.

The chairman of the Federal Reserve Board has presented his concerns and suggested how we can avoid the approaching economic "perfect storm." But the real financial time bomb continues to tick.

Your large pension plan may not make it since the PBGC (Pension Benefit Guaranty Corporation) might go bankrupt. The government may not have the funds to protect what was promised in the past and increased taxes may cause inflation to rise. It is no longer news that Social Security and Medicare may go broke. Do not "put all your eggs in one basket" and expect any one organization to make it through the coming financial storm.

To be prepared, it is wise to spread out your assets, some in real estate, the rest in insured investments, guaranteed by the government and insurance companies. True, insuring federal agencies and insurance corporations may go under, but at least they made a promise to guarantee your account, whereas your other investment options have already warned that you could lose your money.

I am not suggesting you have to prepare for anarchy by digging a bomb-shelter, nor am I encouraging you to hunker down with an arsenal to protect your home. This is a warning voice to watch for the day when the labor market begins to feel the crunch left by the retiring Baby Boomers and other factors.

I am warning you to have your finances in order, so ***IF*** the economy struggles, at least you will have diversified your assets into investments which may gain in value even if the worth of the dollar changes. If the economy crashes, at least you have a home or plot of land to call your own. The extra non-perishable food you set aside will have been a good decision. If you have wisely invested, listening to your advisor, you will have placed your money in liquid, guaranteed accounts where you can still earn as much as the market will bear.

Then, when the storm is past, and you see the silver lining of a new financial era, you will be ready to take advantage of the opportunities that lie ahead.

Because you prepared you did not fear.

Appendix I

National Bureau of Economic Research - Business Cycle Expansions and Contractions[233]

The NBER does not define a recession in terms of two consecutive quarters of decline in real GDP. Rather, a recession is a significant decline in economic activity spread across the economy, lasting more than a few months, normally visible in real GDP, real income, employment, industrial production, and wholesale-retail sales. For more information, see the latest announcement on how the NBER's Business Cycle Dating Committee chooses turning points in the Economy and its latest memo, dated 07/17/03. The July 1980 trough was announced July 8, 1981. The January 1980 peak was announced June 3, 1980.

The determination that the last contraction ended in November 2001 is the most recent decision of the Business Cycle Dating Committee of the National Bureau of Economic Research.

BUSINESS CYCLE REFERENCE DATES		**DURATION IN MONTHS**			
Peak	**Trough**	**Contraction**	**Expansion**	**Cycle**	
Quarterly dates are in parentheses		*Peak to Trough*	*Previous trough to this peak*	*Trough from Previous Trough*	*Peak from Previous Peak*
	Dec 1854 (IV)	--	--	--	--
June 1857(II)	Dec 1858 (IV)	18	30	48	--
Oct 1860(III)	June 1861 (III)	8	22	30	40
Apr 1865(I)	Dec 1867 (I)	**32**	**46**	**78**	**54**
June 1869(II)	Dec 1870 (IV)	18	18	36	50
Oct 1873(III)	Mar 1879 (I)	65	34	99	52
Mar 1882(I)	May 1885 (II)	38	36	74	101
Mar 1887(II)	Apr 1888 (I)	13	22	35	60
July 1890(III)	May 1891 (II)	10	27	37	40
Jan 1893(I)	June 1894 (II)	17	20	37	30
Dec 1895(IV)	June 1897 (II)	18	18	36	35
June 1899(III)	Dec 1900 (IV)	18	24	42	42
Sept 1902(IV)	Aug 1904 (III)	23	21	44	39
May 1907(II)	June 1908 (II)	13	33	46	56
Jan1910(I)	Jan1912 (IV)	24	19	43	32
Jan1913(I)	Dec 1914 (IV)	23	12	35	36
Aug 1918(III)	Mar 1919 (I)	**7**	**44**	**51**	**67**
Jan1920(I)	July 1921 (III)	18	10	28	17
May 1923(II)	July 1924 (III)	14	22	36	40
Oct 1926(III)	Nov 1927 (IV)	13	27	40	41
Aug 1929(III)	Mar 1933 (I)	43	21	64	34
May 1937(II)	June 1938 (II)	13	50	63	93
Feb 1945(I)	Oct 1945 (IV)	**8**	**80**	**88**	**93**
Nov 1948(IV)	Oct 1949 (IV)	11	37	48	45
July 1953(II)	May 1954 (II)	**10**	**45**	**55**	**56**
Aug 1957(III)	Apr 1958 (II)	8	39	47	49
Apr 1960(II)	Feb 1961 (I)	10	24	34	32
Dec 1969(IV)	Nov 1970 (IV)	**11**	**106**	**117**	**116**
Nov 1973(IV)	Mar 1975 (I)	16	36	52	47
Jan1980(I)	July 1980 (III)	6	58	64	74
July 1981(III)	Nov 1982 (IV)	16	12	28	18
July 1990(III)	Mar 1991(I)	8	92	100	108
Mar 2001(I)	Nov 2001 (IV)	8	120	128	128

Average, all cycles:				
1854-2001 (32 cycles)	17	38	55	56*
1854-1919 (16 cycles)	22	27	48	49**
1919-1945 (6 cycles)	18	35	53	53
1945-2001 (10 cycles)	10	57	67	67
Average, peacetime cycles:				
1854-2001 (27 cycles)	18	33	51	52***
1854-1919 (14 cycles)	22	24	46	47****
1919-1945 (5 cycles)	20	26	46	45
1945-2001 (8 cycles)	10	52	63	63

* 31 cycles ** 15 cycles
*** 26 cycles **** 13 cycles

Figures printed in bold are the wartime expansions (Civil War, World Wars I and II, Korean War, and Vietnam War); the wartime contractions, and the full cycles that include the wartime expansions.

Source: http://www.nber.org/cycles/

Sources: NBER; the U.S. Department of Commerce, Survey of Current Business, October 1994, Table C-51.

Appendix II

One Big Happy(?) Family

In an overly simplistic illustration, the economy is almost as complex as a traditional family. The family (or the economy) is often happy, sad, or mad, depending on how the children act with each other. However, in this dynamic, emotional relationship, Mom and Dad are on the board of directors in charge of the family store with their teenage children working as the employees. Mom and Dad make the rules and it is the children who are responsible to bring in the money for the family. The kids get to keep "all" of their income after they pay up to 50% of what they make through a family allowance (or tax). It's not all bad for these working children because Mom and Dad do give money back to the kids as special benefits.

Mom's job is to be in charge of the fiscal policy, and one that she normally enjoys, because she gets to go to the family store and purchase food and clothing. Mom and is often the one responsible to keep the kids busy, and at the same time encourage them to bring in money for the family. She uses an old fashioned approach, and will normally try to be a positive influence by persuading them to go to work by giving them more money through decreasing the allowance they are supposed to pay the family.

Dad, on the other hand (who is responsible for the monetary policy), is left with the budget, figuring out how much money is needed, and the unpopular decisions of occasionally cutting back on spending, as well as trying to find new ways to make money from the children for the family's needs. Both Mom and Dad, with very different personalities (setting the fiscal and monetary policies), are essential, but are not always harmonious, nor do they get everything done at the same time.

When it comes to the teenage siblings (named Inflation and Unemployment), they normally like Mom because she is a little more indulgent (as long as they do their work). But when the kids start to fight over who gets to use the car (one of the many benefits provided by the parents), Mom throws up her hands, and Dad has to step in and often make the unpopular decisions, such as having the family allowance raised or reducing the amount of benefits the teens get. These young people normally like Dad until he has to take control of the situation.

Now, these teens, like most kids, do not see eye to eye. Unemployment, with a little resentment, takes direction from his sibling, Inflation. He likes to make money, but every once in a while, after he has done all the work Inflation has asked of him, is let go from his job, so now he has to rely on the benefits Mom is willing to provide.

Mom and Dad have learned that they need to balance the amount of work and relaxation their children do. Inflation does well as long as she doesn't work too hard. In the past, the family has seen Inflation get sick when she over works, because Unemployment isn't working, and Dad has had to increase taxes on Inflation just to keep the benefits flowing.

Dad also uses a more authoritarian approach. He will often increase the amounts the kids pay the family at different times for different reasons. Normally Dad wants Unemployment to have a break now and then because he knows if Inflation keeps driving Unemployment he will eventually refuse to work. So, as long as she tries to make more money, Dad will require her to pay more allowances.

Family discord comes when Mom and Dad run out of ideas how to keep everyone happy. Occasionally the two of them realize they have to speak with Grandpa (the Chairman of the Federal Reserve Board) to get his guidance. He normally increases or decreases the value of the dollar by changing the interest rates the family receives from its investments or spends for the money it borrows.

Just as happens with many families, this interrelationship is very complex and can have a meltdown at any time. It requires patience and long-suffering on everyone's part and has no simple cookie-cutter answer.

Appendix III

Paying Off Your Home and The Two Week Mortgage Payment Rip-Off

My challenge to you: Plan on *someday* using your retirement money to make a lump sum payment on your home mortgage.

But do not put the extra money into your principal, at least not right away! There is no reason to have the bank earn interest on your extra payments. It is much better for you to put it into a savings or investment account, earn interest on it, and then, when you have enough saved up, pay off your mortgage in one lump sum.

If your bank has sold you on making mortgage payments on a two week basis so you can "pay off your principal faster," STOP! Don't do it, unless your amortization schedule has it figured in for a 25, 20, or 15 year loan. Avoid the bank's plan and you can save tens of thousands of dollars.

On the face, it may sound like a good plan, but in the long run, making early principal payments without it being figured into the amortization schedule is a horrible idea for your finances. There is a better alternative.

Don't get me wrong. It is a good idea to pay off your home. When it comes to financial security, there are few things more satisfying than to know your home is paid for. But don't jump immediately into accepting everything your bank asks of you, especially the every two-week mortgage rip-off.

Check into the facts and see if the bank is getting more benefit out of the plan than you are. It may be just another way for the bank to make money without passing the benefit along to you. This "scam" is where the fat cat bankers make money on your account while you don't make a dime of interest.

Take the money and invest it. When you have enough in your account, and the economy looks like you can invest more, make the commitment and pay off your remaining mortgage in one lump sum.

One website honestly dispels the benefits of the bi-weekly mortgage plan:

> "<u>Myths and advantages</u>
> Savvy consumers need to understand what biweekly mortgage programs will and will not do for them. Here are two common misunderstandings:
> Myth No. 1: Paying your mortgage twice a month gives you better credit. Wrong. Banks often use an automatic

bank draft for their biweekly plans, which means all your mortgage payments will be made on time -- and that will help your credit. But you can get the same effect on a monthly plan using electronic bill paying or an automatic bank draft.
Myth No. 2: Paying twice a month reduces the compound interest on your mortgage.

Wrong. In fact, even though you are paying biweekly, chances are your loan servicing institution is paying your loan monthly. Which means that if you buy into a biweekly plan, you are actually loaning the servicing company half of your mortgage payment -- interest free -- for at least two weeks every month.

What will chop away at your interest are the two additional half-payments going toward the principal each year. In other words, by making 26 payments of half your mortgage, you are in effect making 13 monthly payments instead of the customary 12.

Depending on the terms of your loan -- and who you ask -- one extra payment a year will enable you to pay for your house an average of six to eight years ahead of schedule.

The price tag: Biweekly payment programs are easy, but the convenience comes at a cost. Many lenders offer two ways to pay: upfront or as you go.

> Of the top five mortgage-servicing institutions, four charge enrollment fees that range from $295 to $379. Three also levy additional charges on every transaction. If you want to pay as you go -- without the hefty upfront charge -- fees from the same top five servicers average from $4 to $9 a month."[234]

The example considered a mortgage loan of $150,000, over 30 years, at 7% interest. Rather than making 26 bi-weekly payments, with the excess being credited to the mortgage principal, it would be better to save or invest the money and make some interest on it, rather than allowing the bank to make money on your payments. If invested in a brokerage account earning an average of 8%, you would save $38,967, and if you paid your mortgage off at that time, you would have paid your home off nearly 4-1/2 years sooner, at 23 years, rather than 27-1/2 years.

In conclusion, take the extra money you would have paid on a two week plan, put it in a investment or savings account, and when your investment reaches your decreasing mortgage balance, pay off your loan in one lump sum. You will have earned money on your excess principal payments and paid off the mortgage even faster.

Appendix IV

Securities Sales Charges or Commissions
Much of the cost of making money depends on how involved you are with your portfolio. Investment Advisors have a number of ways to be paid for their advice. Depending on the service, you may be charged up front or the fee may be withheld from your investment.

Security investors with small amounts of money are best served by diversifying their funds into mutual funds. Once you have a larger amount to invest ($25,000 or more) then "fee based" accounts make sense.

The following information is simplified and only highlights the basic information, so, if you want to understand everything about your account, I encourage you to obtain the appropriate document and read the fine print.

Load and No-Load Funds are two different types of funds available from Mutual Fund companies. The "Load" fund is provided through registered representatives and investment advisors who are going to charge a commission to help you choose which of the thousands of funds are the best for your investment style. "No-Load" funds are often more familiar. Rather than paying a broker a commission to introduce you to a fund, the No-Load fund companies will pay out large amounts of money for advertising to get your attention.

Either way, the mutual fund will also charge some other hidden M&E fee (Management and Expense fee) that varies between .15% to more than 3%, and this does not take into consideration the sales charges. You should not purchase a mutual fund totally dependent on whether or not the fund is "cheap". Often, you pay for what you get. For example, a No-Load "Growth" Fund will not always be a better investment than a "Growth" fund which levies a sales charge in a Load fund. It is prudent to spend "due diligence" reviewing the best funds available. There is a lot of work required to compare funds. This is one of the main reasons the majority of investors will ask for help from a professional.

When it comes to Load Funds many mutual fund investors have very little understanding about the difference between A, B, and C Shares. Be aware that each company has different ways of charging their fees, so you will want to read through the prospectus if you would like to understand what is happening with your money.

An "A Share" is usually purchased in larger amounts. Break-points are available at lump sums which require the broker to give discounts depending on the amount invested within a particular "fund family" or company. The benefit of an "A Share" is that once you have purchased a fund there are no more sales charges to get out of the fund. The negative is that there is a usually sizeable fee, often 4% to 5% in one lump sum up front. This definitely encourages the "buy and hold" philosophy. Yet most companies do provide an opportunity to exchange or transfer the fund within their company without any additional fees being charged.

"B Shares" are designed to encourage investors to stay with a particular investment company with no up-front sales charge. Purchased in smaller increments, "B Shares" do not charge a sales commission up front and decrease on a yearly basis. The contingent sales charge starts out at 4% to 5% or more, and over a five to eight year period drops to zero. For example, if you take your money out in the first year you will be charged the full amount, but if you hold the fund with the same company throughout the period of time, you can take your money out and pay no sales charge. Also, there are small annual ¼ point fees that are charged each year. Called "12-b1" fees, these hidden charges can add up over time.

"C Shares" sales charges come in smaller amounts, usually 1% every year. Over time it is more costly to have a "C Share," however, the cost is designed for people who think they might want the money in a short period or time, or if they would want the flexibility to sell in a shorter period of time and not be charged. A one percent in year one is much better than a five percent charge in year one.

Most wise investors recognize that **Fee Based Accounts** are an effective way to receive professional help and save on sales charges. Designed for active involvement, a fee is charged based on the total balance in the account. The more invested, or the more it grows, the lower the percentage. The fees range from about 2.5% to ½% and is split between the Wall Street firm which trades the securities, the broker/dealer which is the "traffic cop" overseeing the transactions, and the investment advisor or broker which gets paid for their investment advice. It takes most investors a little while to get used to fee based accounts, because every little charge and transaction is normally reported to them. The benefit to the account owner is what the federal government likes: full disclosure.

Brokerage Accounts are straightforward securities accounts where investors can hold a variety of investments: cash, money markets, checking accounts, FDIC insured brokered bank CD's, bonds, stocks, mutual funds, annuities, etc. The trading company, or firm, charges the broker for each transaction, so those costs will normally be passed along to the investor. Mutual fund and annuity companies make their money in their management and expense fees that they charge behind the scene. Those charges are only divulged in the thick, legal documents called a "prospectus". The "load" sales charges come out of the investment and are paid directly to the advisor. Bank CD's, bonds and other similar investments will also pay a small fee to the broker.

Stocks and bonds are not the most effective investment when purchased in small amounts. If you purchase $1,000 of a particular stock, the minimum ticket charge may be about $50.00. You would have to earn a 5% return just to break even.

You also do not want to actively trade your stocks in a regular brokerage account. For example, a one or two per cent sales charge, while seemingly low, can eat up all your profits if you buy and sell just two times in a year. At one percent, buy and sell twice means a 4% charge. At a two percent sales fee, with four transactions, you have now spent 8%, and at two and a half percent you have now paid 10%. That may be all you can make in a good year. Also, watch out for some brokers who attempt to "churn" an account, or sell stock a few times in a slow year, so they can make larger commissions. If caught, the broker can be fined by the SEC.

Direct Ownership

Some investors save a few dollars buying and selling securities directly through the individual company. Cutting out the middleman saves "ticket" charges and sales commissions paid to the broker, broker/dealer and trading firm. There is a certain amount of pride to hold in your hand a stock certificate. But in the end, it is still a piece of paper representing the actual ownership of a company with offices thousands of miles away.

There are downsides to direct ownership, though. First, you are at the mercy of the company and its staff to process your transaction. Some of the large companies are quick to respond, but many do not have the staff needed to react as quickly as you would like. A few weeks delay in a volatile market can mean the loss of a sizable amount of money. In addition, it can become complex, keeping track of a diversified portfolio can be an administrative headache. Waiting for dozens of reporting forms at income tax preparation time, keeping track of cost basis, spending valuable time entering the information in your own books, all add up to good reasons to pay for a broker, their advice, the checks and balances provided by their compliance department, and the computerized reports each month, quarter and year-end.

Index of Charts & Illustrations

Sources

1 Greenspan, Alan, Chairman, Federal Reserve Board, Report given before the Federal Reserve Bank of Kansas City Symposium, Jackson Hole, Wyoming, August 27, 2004, Available from www.federalreserve.gov/boarddocs/speeches/
2 Goodman, Dr. Robert, Senior Economist, Putnam Investments, presentation before the AIG Advisor Group 2001 National Education Business Conference, October 6, 2001, Atlanta, Georgia.
3 Campbell, John Y. and Robert J. Shiller, Valuation Ratios and the Long-Term Stock Market Outlook: An Update, Cowles Foundation Discussion Paper No. 1295, Yale University, March 2001, Available from cowles.econ.yale.edu/behfin/2003-04/0311-pollet.pdf
4 Greenspan, Alan, Chairman, Federal Reserve Board, "The Challenge of Central Banking in a Democratic Society," December 5, 1996, www.federalreserve.gov/boarddocs/speeches/1996/
5 Roosevelt, Franklin D., Inaugural Address, March 4, 1933, as published in Samuel Rosenman, ed., The Public Papers of Franklin D. Roosevelt, Volume Two: The Year of Crisis, 1933 (New York: Random House, 1938), pages 11–16.
6 Ibid, Rosenman. pages 11-16.
7 Buffett, Warren E., America's Growing Trade Deficit Is Selling the Nation Out From Under Us. Here's a Way to Fix the Problem—And We Need to Do It Now. Fortune Magazine, http://www.fortune.com/fortune/investing/articles/0,15114,525644,00.html
8 Vincent, Hannah, Stage and screen, Film Review, from in Exepose, Available from

http://xnet.ex.ac.uk/activities/media/exepose/page.php?page=148
9 Religion, The World Almanac and Book of Facts 1995, World Almanac
10 Matthew 24:36, New Testament, Holy Bible, King James Version
11 United States Stock Prices Chart is a composite of the Dow Jones Industrial Average from 1920 to 2004, Cowles Commission provided by Yale University, 1880-1920, and the Foundation for the Study of Cycles, 1789 to 1880.
12 The Elliott Wave Theory, Available from www.elliottwave.com
13 Campbell and Shiller, Valuation Ratios
14 Ibid.
15 The Navigator Report, Fourth Quarter 2001, Clark Capital Management Group, Inc.
16 Ibid.
17 Ibid.
18 Goodman, AIG Advisor Group presentation
19 www.CBSNews.com, Report, "Greenspan Issues Deficit Warning" August 12, 2003, Available from www.cbsnews.com/
20 Ibid.
21 Greenspan, Kansas City Symposium, Jackson Hole
22 "Financing Long-Term Care for the Elderly," Chapter 2, Congressional Budget Office, April 2004, www.cbo.gov
23 U.S. Census Department, Numerical Growth, Available from http://www.census.gov/prod/1/pop/p23-190/p23190-f.pdf
24 World Population Ageing: 1950-2050, United Nations, Department of Economic and Social Affairs, Population Division, Available from www.un.org/esa/population/
25 Ibid.
26 Telcos and European Demographics, Boardwatch: Analysis of Sofware, Services and Stragegy, 03/25/03, Available from http://www.boardwatch.com/
27 Japan: At the Mercy of Demographics, 4/2/03, Available from http://www.boardwatch.com/document.
28 World Population Ageing: 1950-2050, United Nations
29 U.S. Census, Numerical Growth
30 Ibid.
31 U.S. Bureau of the Census, Decennial Censuses for specified years and Population Projections of the United States by Age,

Sex, Race, and Hispanic Origin: 1993 to 2050, Current Population Reports, P25-1104, U. S. Government Printing Office, Washington, DC, 1993. Data for 1990 from 1990 Census of Population and Housing, CPH-L-74, Modified and Actual Age, Sex, Race, and Hispanic Origin Data.
32 Ibid.
33"Financial services industry is facing a labor shortage," Investment News, May 24, 2004, Crain Communications Inc., Detroit MI
34 "The Older Population: Discover This Growing market for Small Business," Isabel M. Isidro, Available from http://www.powerhomebiz.com/vol12/oldmarket.htm
35 The Graying of America, New York State Coalition for Aging, Inc., www.coalitionforaging.org/BudgetAdvocacy1102.pdf
36 U.S. Census, Numerical Growth
37 Evans, Denis A., M.D., and colleagues of Rush-Presbyterian-St. Luke's Medical Center in Chicago. August 2003 issue of the Archives of Neurology, Available from http://www.seniorjournal.com
38 "Financing Long-Term Care for the Elderly," Chapter 2, Congressional Budget Office, April 2004, Available from http://www.cbo.gov/
39 Ibid., Chapter 2
40 Ibid.
41 Coombes, Andrea, April 25, 2004, "Double-Identity Generation," Available from http://cbs.marketwatch.com
42 Ibid.
43 National Center for Policy Analysis, Available from http://www.ncpa.org/studies/s220/s220a.html
44 A Summary of 2004 Annual Reports, Social Security and Medicare Boards of Trustees, Available from http://www.ssa.gov/OACT/TRSUM/trsummary.html
45 National Center for Policy Analysis, Available from http://www.ncpa.org/studies/s220/s220a.html
46 Horton, Jan, "Greenspan Validates Concerns," National Association of Working People, Volume No. II, Issue No. 6, December 1997,
47 Goodman, AIG Advisor Group presentation.
48 Tokyo Stock Exchange Index, Available from http://quote.tse.or.jp/tse/quote.

49 Monetary and Fiscal Policy, International Information Programs, June 2004, Available from http://usinfo.state.gov/products/pubs/oecon/chap7.htm

50 "Greenspan cautiously optimistic. Central bank chairman says US economy poised for eventual rebound, though risks remain." May 21, 2003. Available from money.cnn.com

51 "Uncharted waters": Available from http://usinfo.state.gov/products/pubs/oecon/c ; "opaque": Available from www.CBSNews. Greenspan Issues Deficit Warning August 12, 2003 091525.htm hap7.htm; "sketchy" from remarks by Chairman Alan Greenspan, Globalization and innovation, Conference on Bank Structure and Competition, Federal Reserve Bank of Chicago, Chicago, Illinois, (via satellite), May 6, 2004, Available from www.federalreserve.com

52 "The New Frontier of Retirement Cash Flow Management: Risks and Challenges for the Financial Services Industry," a study by Ernst and Young, 2003, Available from http://www.worksite.net/101503cashflow.pdf

53 Available from a public affairs site from the U. S. State Department, http://usinfo.state.gov/products/pubs/oecon/chap7.htm

54 www.CBSNews. "Greenspan Issues Deficit Warning" August 12, 2003

55 Barnhart, Jo Anne B., Commissioner, Social Security Administration, "Your Social Security Statement," Form SSA-7005-SM-S1(01-2004),

56 A Summary of 2004 Annual Reports, Social Security and Medicare Boards of Trustees

57 Ibid.

58 Social Security Administration 2004 OASDI Trustees Report, "Stochastic Projections," http://www.ssa.gov/OACT/TR/TR04/VI_stochastic.html

59 Natalia, Galina N., Leonid A. Gavrilov, Galina N. Evdokushkina, Victoria G. Smeyonova, EARLY-LIFE PREDICTORS OF HUMAN LONGEVITY: ANALYSIS OF THE XIXth CENTURY BIRTH COHORTS by, ANNALES DE DÉMOGRAPHIE HISTORIQUE 2003, n° 2 p. 177 à 198, Available from http://longevity-science.org/Early-Life-Predictors-2003.pdf

60 National Center for Policy Analysis

61 Ibid.
62 and Medicare Boards of Trustees
63 Ibid.
64 Ibid.
65 Ibid.
66 National Center for Policy Analysis
67 Social Security amendments of 1983, H.R. 1900/P.L. 98-21 (Enacted April 20, 1983), Available from http://www.ssa.gov/history/1983amend2.html
68 A Summary of 2004 Annual Reports, Social Security
69 Ibid.
70 Goodman, AIG Advisor Group
71 Ibid, Goodman
72 "Living in Youngstown, Ohio during the Great Depression An Interview with Steve S." (interviewed by Monica Skordilis), Available from etc.sccoe.org/I99/I99Prj/SS/prime/text/depressionSkordilis.htm
73 Greenspan, Alan, Chairman, Federal Reserve Board, Globalization and Innovation, at the Conference on Bank Structure and Competition, sponsored by the Federal Reserve Bank of Chicago, Chicago, Illinois (via satellite), May 6, 2004, Available from http://federalreserve.gov/boarddocs/speeches
74 "The Current Economic Recession: How Long, How Deep, and How Different From the Past?" January 10, 2002 CRS Report for Congress, Congressional Research Service, The Library of Congress, Available from policy.house.gov/assets/es-currenteconomicresession.pdf
75 Ibid.
76 Ibid.
77 Carlson, Mark, "Causes of Bank Suspensions in the Panic of 1893," Federal Reserve Board, Available from http://www.federalreserve.gov/pubs/feds/2002/200211/200211pap.pdf
78 Joint Economic Committee Report, March 1997, The Importance of the Federal Reserve as quoted from "The Science (and Art) of Monetary Policy," FRBSF Economic Letter, Number 2001-13, May 4, 2001, Available from http://www.house.gov/jec/fed/fed/fed-im; "Compensation from before World War I through the Great Depression,"

by Robert VanGiezen and Albert E. Schwenk, Bureau of Labor Statistics Available from www.stats.bls.gov/opub/cwc/print/cm20030124ar03p1.htm
79 Ibid.
80 Available at www.variety.com
81 Available at http://www.boxofficemojo.com/alltime/adjusted/
82 VanGiezen, Robert and Albert E. Schwenk, "Compensation from before World War I through the Great Depression," Bureau of Labor Statistics www.stats.bls.gov/opub/cwc/print/cm20030124ar03p1.htm
83 Ibid., and numerous personal stories from people who lived through the Depression, and who saw many unemployed families in certain communities, such as Steve S., as quoted above, Living in Youngstown , Ohio during the Great Depression,
84 White, Douglas, "Self-Organizing Systems: The Emergence of Order", New York: Plenum., and "Thermodynamic Principles for the Social Sciences: An introduction to self-organizing systems," F.E.Yates, Ed. 1987, As quoted from, http://eclectic.ss.uci.edu/~drwhite/Anthro179a/ThermodynamicPrinciples.htm
85 "Monetary and Fiscal Policy," Public Affairs site provided by Department of State, Available from http://usinfo.state.gov/products/pubs/oecon/chap7.htm
86 Bouzou, Nicolas, "The Return of Stagflation," [Posted March 13, 2003], Available from http://www.mises.org/fullstory.asp?control=1181
87 Monetary and Fiscal Policy, Department of State
88 Greenspan, "Globalization and Innovation"
89 Farm Real Estate Values Continue to Increase, Agricultural Outlook, December 1996, Economic Research Service/USDA http://ers.usda.gov/publications/agoutlook/dec1996/ao236d2.pd
90 Brendsel, Leland C., Chairman and CEO, Freddie Mac, National Association of Real Estate Editors, New York, NY, June 11, 2002, Available from www.freddiemac.com/speeches/brendsel/lb061102.htm
91 Labonte, Marc, "U.S. Housing Prices: Is There a Bubble? Government and Finance Division, Analyst in Macroeconomics, May 16, 2003, Available from www.firstgov.com,

http://boozman.house.gov/UploadedFiles/Housing%20-%20Is%20There%20a%20Bubble.pdf
92 Ibid.
93 Consumer Price Index, Available from http://stats.bls.gov/cpi/#overview
94 Ibid., U.S. Housing Prices,
95 Ibid.
96 Ibid.
97 Greenspan, Alan, "Monetary policy and the economic outlook," Testimony Before the Joint Economic Committee, U.S. Congress, April 17, 2002, Available from http://www.federalreserve.gov/BOARDDOCS/TESTIMONY/2002/20020417/default.htm
98 Evans, Blanche, "The Perfect Real Estate Storm," Realty Times, http://realtytimes.com/
99 Pender, Kathleen, "Alarm over price of homes," SFGate.com,
100 Bérubé, Gérard, CAmagazine, The Canadian Institute of Chartered Accountants. December 2003, Available from www.camagazine.com/index.cfm/ci_id/18176/la_id/1.htm
101 Ibid.
102 Kellner, Irwin, "ARMs tie the Fed's hands, Rates can't go up without more jobs," CBS MarketWatch.com, Feb. 3, 2004 Available from http://cbs.marketwatch.com/news/story
103 Nothaft, Frank E., The Next Decade for Mortgage Finance, Special Commentary from the Office of the Chief Economist, Freddie Mac's chief economist, June 23, 2004, Available from http://www.freddiemac.com/news/finance/commentary/sp-comm_062304.html
104 Evans
105 Households and Families: 2000, Issued September 2001, http://www.census.gov/prod/2001pubs/c2kbr01-8.pdf, and http://factfinder.census.gov/servlet/
106 U.S. Census Bureau, Historical Census of Housing Tables Living Alone, http://www.census.gov
107 Hamilton, Bob, "The Influence of Demographic Trends on Housing Demand in the United States: A Descriptive Analysis," University of Florida, Department of Geography, April 1, 2004, http://www.clas.ufl.edu/users/rahamilt/pdf/
108 Leamer, Edward, Dr., UCLA Anderson Forecast, June 22, 2004, uclaforecast.com/contents/archive/media_6_04_1.asp

109 Greenspan, Alan, Chairman, Federal Reserve Board, the Meetings of the American Economic Association, San Diego, California, January 3, 2004, federalreserve.gov/boarddocs/speeches/2004/20040103/
110 Kopecki, Dawn, Dow Jones Newswire, "Senate Banking Chair: GSE Bill to Set Insolvency Process," Feb 25, 2004
111 Ely, Bert, "The Federal Financial Sector Safety Net, An Overview of the Issues," March 2001, Executive Summary, Available from
http://www.fsround.org/PDFs/elypaper.PDF, , www.ft.com, www.democrats.com
112 Kopecki
113 Federal Reserve Bank of San Francisco, Economic Letter 2001-29, What is a Recession? Has a Recession Already Started?, Available from http://www.frbsf.org/publications/economics/letter/2001/el2001-29.html
114 FDIC Roundtable on Deposit Insurance Reform, Available from http://www.fdic.gov/deposit/insurance/initiative/thomaswharton.pdf
115 Feldman, Ron J. and Rolnick, Arthur J., Fixing FDICIA, A Plan to Address the Too-Big-To-Fail Problem, http://mineaspolisfed.org/pubs/ar/1997/ar1997
116 Seidman, L. William, Chairman, FDIC, as quoted in Clifford F. Thies and Daniel A. Gerlowski, "Deposit Insurance: A History of Failure," Cato Journal, http://www.cato.org/pubs/journal/cj8n3/cj8n3-8.pdf
117 Stern, Gary H., President, Federal Reserve Bank of Minneapolis, Deposit Insurance, "Too-Big-To-Fail And Small Banks," minneapolisfed.org/pubs/fedgaz/98-04/opinion.cfm
118 Wilmarth, Arthur E., Jr., "Controlling Systemic Risk in an Era of Financial Consolidation," Available from www.imf.org/external/np/leg/sem/2002/cdmfl/eng/wilmar.pdf
119 Ibid.
120 Ibid. Wilmarth, as quoting: Thomas M. Hoenig, "Financial Industry Megamergers and Policy Challenges," 84 Economic Review No. 3 (Fed. Res. Bank of K.C., MO), 3d Qtr. 1999, at 7-8, 10-13; Kaufman, On Money and Markets, supra note 19, at 207, 237-38; Remarks by FRB Governor Laurence H. Meyer before a National Bureau of Economic Research Conference, Jan. 14, 2000 (available at

www.federalreserve.gov); Frederic S. Mishkin, "Financial consolidation: Dangers and opportunities," 23 Journal of Banking & Finance 675, 680-81 (1999); Santomero & Eckles, supra note 24, at 15, 18-19; Gary H. Stern, "Thoughts on Designing Credible Policies After Financial Modernization," 14 Region No. 3 (Fed. Res. Bank of Minneapolis, MN), Sept. 2000, at 4-5, 24-25.

121 Ibid.

122 Ibid.

123 Berger, George S., "Reforming Deposit Insurance And The Regulatory System: The Failure Of The Middle Way," The Cato Journal, Volume 14, Number 2, Fall 1994, Available at http://www.cato.org/pubs/journal/cjv14n2-4.html

124 Ely.

125 Berger, George S., "Reforming Deposit Insurance And The Regulatory System: The Failure Of The Middle Way, The Cato Journal, Volume 14, Number 2, Fall 1994, www.cato.org/pubs/journal/cjv14n2-4.html; George G. Kaufman, "The New Safety Net," Loyola University Chicago; and Peter J . Wallison, American Enterprise Institute, "Regulation, Banking and Finance," Summer 2001, The Cato Institute, Available from http://www.cato.org/pubs/journal/cjv14n2-4.html

126 Berger

127 Chu, Kam Hon, "Is Free Banking More Prone to Bank Failures than Regulated Banking?" The Cato Journal, Vol. 16, No. 1, www.cato.org/pubs/journal/cj16n1-3.html

128 Kovacevich, Richard M., "Deposit insurance: It's time to cage the monster," Fedgazette, April 1996, Available at http://minneapolisfed.org/pubs/fedgaz/96-04/edi964b.cfm

129 Federal Reserve Bank of Minneapolis, "Fixing FDICIA, A Plan to Address the To-Big-To-Fail Problem," The Region, 1997 Annual Report Issue,http://minneapolisfed.org/pubs/ar/1997/ar1997.cfm

130 George G. Kaufman, "How Real Is the Risk of a Massive Banking Collapse?" The Cato Institute, Regulation, Volume 23, Number 1, Available at www.cato.org/pubs/regulation/regv23n1/kaufman.pdf

131 Bank Failure, An Evaluation of the Factors Contributing to the Failure of National Banks, Comptroller of the Currency,

Administrator of National Banks, Washington, D.C. , June 1988, Available at http://www.occ.treas.gov/bankfailure.pdf

132 England, Catherine, "Are Banks Special?," The Cato Institute, Regulation, Volume 14, Number 2, Spring 1991, Available at http://www.fdic.gov/bank/analytical/regional/ro20041q/na/infocus.html

133 Committee on Education and the Workforce, Democratic Staff, US House of Representatives, Enron Administrative Committee minutes, www.house.gov/eeo_democrats/enroninfo.html

134 Hawke, John D. Jr., Comptroller of the Currency Before the Subcommittee on Financial Institutions and Consumer Credit of the Committee on Financial Services of the United States House of Representatives, July 26, 2001, Available at http://www.occ.treas.gov/ftp/release/2001-67b.txt

135 Morgan, Donald P., "Rating Banks: Risk and Uncertainty in an Opaque Industry," Federal Reserve Board of New York, April 2000, Available at http://www.ny.frb.org/research/economists/morgan/draft9.pdf

136 Ibid.

137 Kaufman, George, "Deposit Insurance," The Concise Encyclopedia of Economics, Available at http://www.econlib.org/library/Enc/DepositInsurance.html

138 Farrell, Chris, "FDIC Reform: Use the Market to Monitor Big Banks," Federal Reserve Bank of Minneapolis, June 2000, As Found at http://woodrow.mpls.frb.fed.us/pubs/region/00-06/farrell.cfm

139 Greenspan, "Globalization and Innovation." At the Conference on Bank Structure and Competition, sponsored by the Federal Reserve Bank of Chicago, Chicago, Illinois, (via satellite), May 6, 2004

140 FDIC Study: Implications of Housing Market Boom, Press Release, http://www.fdic.gov/news/news/press/2004/pr1704.html

141 Kaufman, George, Central Banks, Asset Bubbles, and Financial Stability, Research Department, Federal Reserve Bank of Chicago, (WP-98-12) www.chicagofed.org

142 Ibid.

143 White, Lawrence, J., 1990-Regulation, The Cato Review of Business & Government, Currents, NYU Stern, School of

Business, Available at http://www.cato.org/pubs/regulation/regv13n1/reg13n1-currents.html
144 Kaufman.
145 Options Paper, August 2000, Federal Deposit Insurance Corporation, Available at www.fdic.gov/deposit/insurance/initiative/OptionPaper.html
146 Ibid.
147 Ibid.
148 FDIC Statistics on Despoitory Institutions, Available at http://www2.fdic.gov/sdi/main4.asp
149 Kaufman, George G., "The New Safety Net," Loyola University Chicago, and Peter J. Wallison, American Enterprise Institute, Regulation, Banking and Finance, Summer 2001, The Cato Institute, Available at http://www.cato.org/pubs/regulation/regv24n2/kaufman.pdf
150 Ibid.
151 Ibid.
152 Miller, Rae-Ann, and Jeffrey Ayres, "Federal Deposit Insurance Corporation, FYI: An Update on Emerging Issues in Banking, Could a Bull Market Be a Panacea for Defined Benefit Pension Plans?" January 13, 2004, Available at http://www.fdic.gov/bank/analytical/fyi/2004/011304fyi.html
153 Ibid.
154 "Performance and Accountability Report," Pension Benefit Guaranty Corporation, Fiscal Year 2004, November 15, 2004, http://www.pbgc.gov/publications/annrpt/PAR1104.pdf
155 Ibid.
156 ibid.
157 Belt, Bradley B., Executive Director, Pension Benefit Guaranty Corporation, Presentation to the 6th Annual Conference of the Retirement Research Consortium, August 13, 2004, Available at http://www.pbgc.gov/news/speeches/sp081304.thm
158 Miller and Ayres.
159 Ibid.
160 Ibid.
161 Manor, Robert and Christopher Steiner. "Steel Mill Retirees Feel Pinch From Caps," Chicago Tribune, November 5, 2003.
162 Miller and Ayres

163 Belt
164 Baker, Richard, Representative, "GSE Oversight: The Need for Reform and Modernization," U.S. House of Representatives, Subcommittee on Capital Markets, Insurance and Government Sponsored Enterprises Committee on Financial Service, June 25, 2003, Available at http://commdocs.house.gov/committees/bank/hba91771.000/hba91771_0.HTM
165 U.S. Department of State, International Information Program, Fact Sheet: The Charges Against International Terrorist Usama Bin Laden, Available at http://usinfo.state.gov/topical/pol/terror/99129502.htm
166 Kurata, Phillip, "Islamic Scholars Reject Bin Laden's Call for Jihad Against Americans" (Denunciations from N. America, Europe, Middle East, South Asia), Washington File Staff Writer, Available at usembassy.state.gov/posts/pk1/wwwh01101902.html
167 http://dictionary.reference.com/search?q=nihilism
168 Krauthammer, Charles, "They Hate Civilization," New York Post, October 16, 2001, Available at http://www.mideasttruth.com/nyp1.html also printed in "The Enemy is Not Islam: It is Nihilism," The Weekly Standard, Available at http://www.weeklystandard.com/Content/Public/Articles/000/000/000/364llkga.asp
169 Garber, Seth, M.D., "A Perfect Storm: Rising Health Care Costs," Health Care Crisis, Oregon School Boards Association, 2004, http://www.osba.org/hotopics/hlthcare/storm.htm
170 Confronting the New Health Care Crisis: Improving Health Care Quality and Lowering Costs By Fixing Our Medical Liability System, U.S. Department of Health and Human Services, Office of the Assistant Secretary for Planning and Evaluation July 25, 2002, Available at http://aspe.hhs.gov/daltcp/reports/litrefm.htm
171 Content, Thomas, "Automakers Shift Focus to Health Care Crisis," Milwaukee Journal Sentinel, August 9, 2004
172 A Summary of 2004 Annual Reports, Social Security and Medicare Boards of Trustees, Available at http://www.ssa.gov/OACT/TRSUM/trsummary.html

173 Confronting the New Health Care Crisis: U.S. Department of Health and Human Services, http://aspe.hhs.gov/daltcp/reports/litrefm.htm
174 Ibid.
175 US Census, 2004 Publication, wp02-1
176 Ibid.
177 Ibid
178 Ibid.
179 Ibid.
180 Greenspan, Kansas City Symposium, Jackson Hole
181 Ibid.
182 Martin, Jack, "Immigration Run Amok: Why We Need Reform, Current policies do not meet America's national needs and fuel an undesirable population increase," American Foreign Service Association, Available at http://www.afsa.org/fsj/jun01/martinjune01.cfm
183 Ibid.
184 "Why Americans Support Immigration Reform, Federation for American Immigration Reform," Available at http://209.25.133.193/html/04146710.htm
185 Numerical Growth, US Census, Page 2-2, Available at http://www.census.gov/prod/1/pop/p23-190/p23190-f.pdf
186 Lazarus, Emma, The New Colossus, Available at http://alpha.furman.edu/~ateipen/lazarus.html
187 World in the Balance: The People Paradox, NOVA, Public Broadcasting System, April 20, 2004, Available at http://www.pbs.org/wgbh/nova/transcripts/3108_worldbal.html
188 Drought, National Oceanic and Atmospheric Administration, Available at http://www.drought.noaa.gov
189 Population and Demographics, Arizona Department of Commerce, Available at http://www.commerce.state.az.us/prop/eir/popanddemo.asp
190 California's Population, Public Policy Institute of California, April 2003, Available at http://www.ppic.org/content/pubs/JTF_PopulationJTF.pdf and Census Bureau, http://www.census.gov/prod/2001pubs/c2kbr01-2.pdf, Ibid
191 Drought, NOAA
192 Krist, John, "Drought boosts campaign to drain one of the West's biggest reservoirs," Friday, August 27, 2004,

Environmental News Network (ENN), Available at http://www.enn.com/news/2004-08-27/s_26723.asp
193 Johnson, Kirk, and Dean Murphy, "Drought Settles In, Lake Shrinks and West's Worries Grow," New York Times, May 2, 2004, Available at http://www.newyorktimes.com or http://forests.org/articles/reader.asp
194 Climatic Fluctuations, Drought, and Flow in the Colorado River Basin, U.S. Department of the Interior, U.S. Geological Survey, USGS Fact Sheet 2004-3062, version 2, August 2004, Available at water.usgs.gov/pubs/fs/2004/3062/#fig3
195 Ibid.
196 Johnson and Murphy, Drought Settles In
197 Krist.
198 Study: Global Warming Brings Extreme Changes to California, Worst Effects Can be Avoided by Cutting Carbon Dioxide Release, August 17, 2004, Available at http://www.nbcsandiego.com/weather/3660098/detail.html
199 Drought, NOAA
200 Appenzeller, Tim and Dennis R. Dimick, "Signs From Earth," National Geographic Magazine, September 2004
201 Arseneau, David M., Optimal Inflation in an Open Economy with Imperfect Competition, Federal Reserve Board, March, 2004, Available at http://www.federalreserve.gov/pubs/feds/2004/200425/200425pap.pdf
202 Goodman, AIG Advisor Group Presentation
203 Ibid.
204 The Current Economic Recession: How Long, How Deep, and How Different From the Past? Congressional Research Service, The Library of Congress, January 10, 2002, CRS Report for Congress, Available at http://policy.house.gov/assets/es-currenteconomicresession.pdf
205 Greenspan, Kansas City Symposium, Jackson Hole
206 Greenspan, Globalization and Innovation
207 National Bureau of Economic Research - Business Cycle Expansions and Contractions, Available at http://www.nber.org/cycles/
208 The New Frontier of Retirement Cash Flow Management: Risks and Challenges for the Financial Services Industry, a

study by Ernst and Young, 2003, http://www.worksite.net/101503cashflow.pdf

209 Huddle, Dr. Donald, "The Net Costs of Immigration: The Facts, The Trends, and The Critics," Department of Economics, Rice University, October 22, 1996.

210 Ibid.

211 International Information Programs, Monetary and Fiscal Policy, usinfo.state.gov/products/pubs/oecon/chap7.htm Remarks by Chairman Alan Greenspan At the Meetings of the American Economic Association, San Diego, California, January 3, 2004

212 http://www.amateur-investors.com/Causes_of_Stock_Market_Crash_in_1929.htm

213 Greenspan, Alan, Chairman, Federal Reserve Board, "Testimony of Chairman Alan Greenspan, The Economic Outlook, Before the Joint Economic Committee," U.S. Congress, May 21, 2003, Available at www.federalreserve.gov/boarddocs/testimony/2003/20030521/default.htm

214 Greenspan, Kansas City Symposium, Jackson Hole

215 Berner, Dick, Chief U.S. Economist, Morgan Stanley, "FDIC Economist Roundtable Reviews Past, Looks to the Future," 05/13/2003, Available at http://www.fdic.gov/news/conferences/Economists.html

216 National Center for Policy Analysis

217 Goodman, AIG Advisor Group Presentation.

218 Ibid. and, John Y. Campbell and Robert J. Shiller, Valuation Ratios and the Long-Term Stock Market Outlook: An Update, Cowles Foundation Discussion Paper No. 1295, Yale University, March 2001. http://cowles.econ.yale.edu/behfin/2003-04/0311-pollet.pdf

219 Evergreen Quarterly, Evergreen Investment Management Company, LLC, Evergreen Investment Services, Inc., May 2004

220 Goodman, Dr.Robert, Putnam Mutual Funds, Senior Economic Advisor, Retired, literature.putnam.com/literature/pdf/II560.pdf

221 Personal Finance, Money 101, Lesson 5, Stocks, and Lesson 6, Mutual Funds, Available at http://money.cnn.com/pf/101/lessons/5/page2.html

222 The Hartford, The Director Suite of Variable Annuities, A Voyage Through Investment Cycles, DIR704 2/04
223 Ibid.
224 The Hartford, The Director Suite of Variable Annuities, Beyond Investment Illusions, P3320 6/04
225 Ibid
226 Greenspan, Kansas City Symposium, Jackson Hole
227 The Hartford, Beyond Investment Illusions,
228 Huggard, John P., Investing With Variable Annuities, Dispelling The Myths and Misconceptions Surrounding Variable Annuities and Mutual Funds, North Carolina State University, March 23, 2004
229 Fleckenstein, Bill, Contrarian Chronicles, CNBC, http://www.tradewithvision.com/kbase/pdf/contrarian_chronicles.pdf
230 Consumer Price Index (CPI) is an index representing the rate of inflation of U.S. consumer prices as determined by the U.S. Bureau of Labor Statistics based on the cost of a variety of goods and services.
231 The Hartford, Beyond Investment Illusions
232 Benson, Ezra T., Secretary of Agriculture during the Eisenhower Administration, 1953-1961, "Prepare Ye," Ensign Magazine, Intellectual Reserves, Inc., January 1974.
233 National Bureau of Economic Research - Business Cycle Expansions and Contractions, http://www.nber.org/cycles/
234 Available at http://www.bankrate.com/brm/news/mtg/20010920

David Hoefferle is a Financial and Tax Consultant and President of United Financial Center, LLC, located in Tucson, Arizona. He teaches Certified Financial Planning courses at the University of Phoenix.

David was a Hinckley Scholar, graduating summa cum laude from Brigham Young University with a bachelor's degree in Communications. He is a member of the National Association of Tax Practitioners and other professional organizations. He holds several securities registrations and other financial and insurance industry licenses.

David conducts estate and retirement planning seminars and is well known as the producer and host of many television financial news reports. He is a published financial author and is listed in Who's Who. David serves on the boards of large privately funded foundations and is a distinguished lay leader at his church in Tucson, where he and his wife, Rena, make their home. As the father of four children, and as a grandfather, he is concerned with the future of America's economy.